What's Up, Doc?
A Surgeon's Story

DR. RIAZ MOHAMMED

WESTBOW
PRESS®
A DIVISION OF THOMAS NELSON
& ZONDERVAN

WestBow Press books may be ordered through booksellers or by contacting:

WestBow Press
A Division of Thomas Nelson & Zondervan
1663 Liberty Drive
Bloomington, IN 47403
www.westbowpress.com
1 (866) 928-1240

Scripture quotations marked (KJV) taken from the King James Version of the Bible.

ISBN: 978-1-9736-6880-0 (sc)
ISBN: 978-1-9736-6881-7 (hc)
ISBN: 978-1-9736-6879-4 (e)

Library of Congress Control Number: 2019909685

Print information available on the last page.

WestBow Press rev. date: 7/22/2019

To my wife, Janet, and our beloved children, Mark and Sylvia.

ACKNOWLEDGEMENTS

I am most grateful to the Reverend Dr George Mitchell, Mr Barry Sprott, and Dr Norman Wallace for their encouragement, as well as useful advice and assistance in the writing of this autobiography.

CONTENTS

INTRODUCTION

You might ask the reasonable question, "Why are you bothering to write an autobiography?" Well, one reason is that many people, having heard me speak at church meetings over the years—giving my "testimony"— have encouraged me to do so. Since the time available when speaking at church meetings is limited, it has never been possible to tell my "whole story". Hence, writing an autobiography seemed a good way of telling more of my story for those who may be interested.

By its nature, an autobiography requires writing something about your own life story. Whilst this causes no problem for some, I found writing about myself somewhat difficult. I have never found attracting attention to myself in any way desirable and take the view that there are very many more important and interesting things for people to spend their time on than reading about me! However, many people have continued to encourage me to write an autobiography, and finally I have given in.

In addition to the difficulty of writing about oneself and deciding what to put in and what to leave out, I have always had some concerns about what might happen should my autobiography ever be published and become available to the general public. It is, I thought, quite possible that someone may be offended by what I have written—to the extent of taking punitive action against me or my family. How could this be avoided? As I could not come up with any solution to this possibility, except, of course, not publishing, this concern did cause a significant delay in the writing of my autobiography.

However, rightly or wrongly, having made the decision to publish, I can now only hope and pray that anyone reading my story, including my own extended family, will not take anything I have written as a personal criticism. It has, as God knows, never been my intention to cause offence to anyone. As everyone will fully understand, I did not wish to write anything that could cause distress or pain to my beloved parents. As I felt I could not avoid that possibility, I thought it best to refrain from writing anything about my life experiences till they had passed away from this life.

Another reason for the delay in the writing of my autobiography is that I was always keen not to write it "too soon". I thought this would not be wise. I wanted to wait till I felt sure the time was "just right". Being in a busy full-time medical job does not lend itself to having much free time to write autobiographies either, so I made the decision to wait until I had fully retired from work before attempting to write my story.

The most important reason, which remains above all the others, for my writing this autobiography is simply to show what my life is all about in relationship to God. It isn't that my life and walk with God has somehow been perfect in every way; that is simply not so. God knows fully how often I have made mistakes and let Him and others down. It is only through His sovereign grace and mercy that I stand where I stand today.

You might ask me, "What is it that you would wish to convey to those who read your autobiography?" The answer, I hope, is simple and honest. My desire is to encourage everyone who reads my autobiography to seriously consider following Jesus Christ, who is my saviour and Lord. I do not wish to hide in any way this objective. If that were to happen, then I would have simply failed in my main reason for writing this autobiography.

Now that my parents are no longer with us and I have finally retired from work as a medical practitioner, I have a little more "free time" and, hence, less excuse for not writing my autobiography.

Here then is the story of my journey through life. I do hope you enjoy reading it and finding it of some value.

CHAPTER 1

The Early Days

If we had never met and you were to have a telephone conversation with me, you may well conclude from my accent that I must be Scottish in origin. But you would be mistaken!

You may well ask me, as people often do, "So where do you come from?" This question for many is probably quite simple and one to which the answer is confidently given, invoking accepted notions of personal belonging, identity, culture, and even pride.

For me, it's not quite that simple. While I can give the answer, "I come from Gujarat, in Pakistan," this goes only a small part of the way in explaining my origins and identity. In all honesty, I am not sure, even to this day, where I really belong!

I was indeed born in a little-known village called Gujarat. This village was in the district of Gujarat, which forms a part of the province of Punjab in Pakistan. Just to make matters somewhat more confusing for those who do not know the geography of this part of the world, there is another area, many miles away, called the state of Gujarat, which forms part of India and is not in Pakistan. Incidentally, as far as I can remember, for reasons I am not aware of, the whole area around the village was taken over by the US Army.

History informs us that the subcontinent of India received its independence from British rule in 1947. This led to a significant split of India, resulting in the creation of two new countries, known as West

Pakistan and East Pakistan. This happened out of a desire for identity by some people who sought an independent country of their own. The main reason for this was religious differences between Muslims, who were in the minority but wanted an Islamic homeland, and the majority Hindus, who continued to live in India. Sadly, this parting was not at all peaceful. When India broke up, many people had to flee for safety from their homes—either to India if they were Hindus or to Pakistan if they were Muslims.

Subsequently, India became a democratic republic, with West Pakistan and East Pakistan being independent. Though they were many miles apart geographically, they became one Islamic republic. Subsequently, West Pakistan and East Pakistan also separated—with West Pakistan becoming Pakistan and East Pakistan becoming Bangladesh. Unfortunately, these political and religious differences continue to cause significant problems particularly between Pakistan and India.

As I was not yet born when West Pakistan was created, these political and religious differences had no consequences for me. But as I would find out later, my parents were deeply affected.

I was the second eldest of four brothers born into a Muslim family. We did have a sister as well. Sadly, she died when she was very young, and I did not really know her. I do recall, however, that she had severe diarrhoea virtually all the time and was very thin before she died. I wonder now if she had ulcerative colitis or something similar and could have survived with adequate medical care!

Despite my young age, I have retained many memories of my time in the village of Gujarat and can recall vividly some incidents that involved me in one way or another.

We lived in a big house that, I was told, my father had built for the family. It had a basement, a middle floor, and an upper floor. It was bigger, taller, and clearly more expensive to build than any other house in the village. Also, I recall that at the front of the house on the highest floor, at the very top, was the semicircular lunar symbol of Islam. No other house had that. In addition, we had our own water pump in the basement of the house, so we had fresh water always available. This meant that, unlike other children, we had no need to go to the village well to collect water. We were, hence, better off than many others in the village.

I remember on one evening leaving the house on my own for the very first time. I can only imagine I was not much older than three or four years of age. It was a bright warm night with the moon fully visible. All the other children, who were older than me, were running around me, playing, and prancing about, as you would expect. I suppose I may have been part of the attraction that night, being very young and out alone for the first time. I'm not sure how I managed to get out of the house all by myself. Mum would have been horrified if she had seen me escaping the house! I can only imagine the childminder must have been distracted while looking after my elder brother.

I was excited to be out alone and just ran around without any real motivation. Then suddenly, I found myself falling into a pool of dirty water. I knew it was there, as I could see it from my house and was often told to stay away from it, but I had no idea how close it was to the path I was running on. I felt myself falling farther and farther into the water. No one came to my assistance.

I remember trying to hold onto grass at the edge of the pond and trying, with great difficulty, to drag myself out of the pond. I was terrified and remember praying to Allah, even at that young age, for help.

Somehow, I did not drown and did manage to get out—wet and dirty but at least still alive. I went, or was taken, to my granddad's house to get cleaned up before being taken home. I suspect my grandfather came with me not only to ensure that I got home safely but also to avoid me getting punishment for what I had just done. That's granddads for you.

On another occasion, when I was a little older, I remember trying to jump over some barbed wire at the edge of a field. I was just trying to copy the older children, who were doing this for fun. I did not have any shoes on. Unfortunately, I did not manage to clear the barbed wire and sustained a deep cut along the whole front of my right foot. There was much blood everywhere. I was taken home and was attended to by a medical worker. He could not stitch the wound, as he did not have the necessary equipment or the skill to do so. He could only put some antibiotic powder into the wound and bandages around my foot to stop the bleeding.

I do recall lots of the village folk coming to the house watching all this happening to me. Some of the women, I was told, could not bear to look at my foot because of the large wound and the bleeding that it caused. I, apparently, sat quite calmly and patiently and allowed the medical worker to dress the wound. I do remember that it took several weeks for the wound to heal, leaving a great big permanent scar. During this time, I was confined to the house for my own good.

On another occasion, while I was playing upstairs, my mother called me to come down and see something interesting in the basement. I asked what it was, but she refused to tell me and simply ordered me to come down the stairs right away.

Reluctantly, I made my way down to the basement, and what I saw was an absolute delight. We owned some hens, and one of the mother hens had had about twenty chickens just born. These chicks were walking about and making chicken-like noises, with the mother hen protecting them all under her outstretched wings. I did not dare go too near, as I would be facing the wrath of the protective mother hen! It was a wonderful surprise to behold.

I can also recall the occasion when my mum and dad left the house to go to some Muslim celebration elsewhere. I managed to get out of the house, yet again, without my childminder seeing me. I made my way down the village but had no idea where Mum and Dad had gone. I went into a neighbour's house to ask for directions to the feast. I had no idea who the neighbours were. The neighbours said that they did not know where my parents had gone and that my parents would not be pleased if I did not return home. They then gently led me back to my own house and ensured I was safely in the hands of the childminder. I was not at all happy with their actions, thinking that they should have taken me to where my parents had gone.

When Mum and Dad came home, I told them what these "naughty people" had done. The neighbours had refused to take me to see them. To my utter surprise, Mum told me not to criticise them, as they were "good people" and were "Christians".

I had never heard of such people. They clearly had the respect of my mother. Now that I look back on my life, I wonder if they were true believers and prayed for me. I never saw them again. They will not know that I too became a follower of Jesus Christ!

The final recollection I have of my time in the village of Gujarat was an incident that took place during the rainy season. It transpired that a young boy was looking after some cattle on his own just outside the village. One animal went into a fast-flowing stream and ended up in some danger in a deep pond. The boy foolishly went into the pond to help rescue the animal. I recall that, when the message went out that this boy was in danger of drowning, the men of the village went into the pond after him. One of my uncles was involved in the rescue attempt. All the village children watched with some excitement to see what would happen. We were not, of course, allowed to go to the pond. But we all waited in the village centre, expecting them all to come back that way.

The men of the village managed to get the boy out of the water and brought him into the village. We all watched in astonishment as he just lay motionless on the ground, with nobody knowing what to do. His mother and family soon arrived and were naturally upset to see what was happening to him.

Sometime later, a medical worker arrived riding on a bicycle. Without saying any words, he examined the boy's chest with a stethoscope and then just shook his head from side to side indicating that the boy was dead and that nothing more could be done for him. At this, the mother went into a hysterical weeping episode, tearing her hair out. All the other family members and friends also started to weep.

I found that there were tears in my eyes too, and I was asking myself a question: *Why was a doctor not here to help?*

It was at that moment I decided I would become a doctor when I grew up, so that I could help people!

Shortly afterwards, the news filtered out to the family that Dad and Mum had decided we would all be going to live in the United Kingdom. My father had left Pakistan a few years earlier to go to work in Scotland on his own and make a new life possible for us all. It was now time for his family to join him there. This was a complete surprise to me. But, of course, at the age of six, you don't tend to have much of a say as to what plans Mum and Dad have for you! That the political instability of the country had a part to play in the decision seems likely, but not everyone had the choice to move away. It was decided that we would tour round Pakistan saying farewell to grandparents and other relatives before heading for the United Kingdom.

I got the feeling that my paternal grandparents, who were farmers and lived in the village, were not all that keen to see their grandsons leave them, probably for good. However, they did not say too much about it. My other grandparents, who lived in Lahore, seemed more enthusiastic concerning the forthcoming move. My maternal grandfather was an educated person who was a headmaster in a college in Lahore and spoke English well. He seemed to hold the United Kingdom in high regard and was keen to see us move there for a better future.

I remember well the occasion of our actual departure from the village. A horse and cart came to take us into the city to catch a train. The children of the village came out to say goodbye. As expected, all were excited, shouting and screaming at the top of their voices. They all ran after the horse-drawn cart until they could run no more. One young boy outran the others. Then, naturally, as he came to the edge of the village, he had to stop. Before we disappeared around the corner of a field never to meet again, I saw him wave goodbye and say in our native Urdu language, "God be with you!" That incident happened over sixty years ago, but I have not forgotten what that young boy said!

The family, after travelling for a long time on trains came to a town called Bahawalpur, where my father had apparently owned and ran a shop for some years. We stayed there in a house shared with relatives and did not leave for the United Kingdom as soon as I expected.

My elder brother and I started to attend a local school, and for some months, nothing happened. It was sometime later that I discovered that my parents were of two minds as to whether my father, who was in the United Kingdom by this time, should come home or that the rest of the family should join him. Finally, for reasons I did not know, the decision was made for us to join my father in the United Kingdom.

After a long time travelling by train, we arrived in the city called Karachi. We were accompanied by an uncle, who stayed overnight with us in a hotel, before we boarded a plane the next morning to fly to the United Kingdom.

We children were very excited about this great adventure that was about to be undertaken. I had never seen an aeroplane before, never mind gone on one. I could not understand why there were tears in my mother's eyes and those of my uncle's when we parted and boarded the aeroplane.

I did not realise at the time what they must have known and what turned out to be the case—we would never see each other again!

After a long tiring plane journey, which would have been very difficult for Mum—as, by this time, she had four of us boys to look after all by herself—we finally arrived at our father's house in Glasgow.

The house was part of a tenement building in an area of Glasgow known as Bridgeton. The street was called Monteith Row and overlooked a huge park known locally as Glasgow Green. The scenery was spectacular, but unfortunately, the area was not in any way a "healthy" place to live in. It apparently was well known to the police and was a place where prostitutes did a roaring trade. It was not a safe area to walk about in, particularly at night!

An incident comes immediately to mind that typifies what the area we lived in was like at the time. One Saturday afternoon, as I was returning home after playing in a local swing park, I decided to take a shortcut by going down a quieter narrower back lane to my house, rather than going along the front, like I usually did. As I was passing the back door of a neighbour's house, suddenly a young man came out. He was under the influence of alcohol. He grabbed hold of me, took out a very large knife, and held it against my throat. He asked me for my name and, on hearing it, became very aggressive. He wanted to know if I was related to someone whose name sounded like mine. I did not know who he was talking about and simply said so. I was utterly terrified.

As he continued to question me further, a lady, who I recognised as one of the local shopkeepers, opened her back window and tried to intervene. The man, on noticing her, threw his knife at her and started to swear at the same time. Fortunately, the knife missed her and hit the wall and fell onto the ground. He left me to fetch his knife.

I was too terrified to do anything but simply stand still. When he came back with his knife, he had made up his mind that I was telling the truth and was not related to the person with a similar name, whom he obviously hated. He apologised for his actions. We then shook hands, and I walked away. I decided not to go into my house through the back way as intended, so as not to let the man see where I lived. I walked past the house and, at the end of the lane, walked to the front and then made my way home that way. I didn't tell my mum what had happened. There seemed little benefit in doing so. Besides, at the end of the day, I was physically unharmed. That was the kind of area we had to live in.

Though, obviously, the house we lived in was not in a good area, Dad had done quite well acquiring such a property for the family. He was not an educated man and had to make his living working as a labourer on the roads. He was, however, very enterprising and intelligent and had several ideas about projects he wanted to start, with a view to increasing his wealth.

I also found out later that it was very unusual for a man of my father's background to have the privilege of marrying a lady such as my mother, who was born into a highly educated family. She loved reading and writing and wanted to be educated like her brothers. However, as she was a girl, her father would not allow her to progress in learning. As a good Muslim lady, her position was to be in the kitchen learning how to cook. She was not given a choice as far as further education was concerned.

Despite her personal lack of education, it would have been the normal practise for Mum to be given in marriage to a man from another family who were also highly educated. These marriages would be "arranged" marriages, usually planned by parents.

It seems that the Second World War had some part to play in my father and mother's union. My father was a sergeant in the Indian Army and fought with the British Army in Europe. He was captured, together with others, by the Germans. He did, however, manage to escape capture, together with an army officer. That officer was one of my mother's brothers. My father, being of a farming background and a very practical man, was the one mainly responsible for leading my uncle through France and into safety.

After the war, my father met up with his army officer friend in Lahore, where my mother's family lived. It was there that he met my mother for the first time and was immediately attracted to her. He requested my mother's hand in marriage.

This request would not normally have been accepted, given that he was not an educated person and had not gone to university, unlike all my mother's brothers. They were all university educated, and her father was a headmaster. However, because of the close relationship between my father and my mother's brother from their experience during the Second

World War, my uncle supported my father's request, with the result that she was eventually given in marriage to him.

After many years of hard work in various ways, including door-to-door selling of clothing, my father came up with a new idea. He would travel by road in a van all the way to Pakistan and bring back various items for sale in Europe. This, I assume, was a much cheaper way to travel than by plane. This apparently had not been done before. Because of this venture, my father finally set up successful businesses in France and Holland. These businesses consisted of transporting cloth made in Pakistan into Europe for sewing into clothing for sale in a much richer Europe. He used several relatives in these business enterprises, thus helping others from the extended family to immigrate to Europe.

Whilst Dad spent several years travelling back and forth from Pakistan on business ventures, Mum, who remained in Glasgow, became unwell. She was isolated from her own extended family and culture, resulting in the development of a deep depression. We, her sons, had all grown up and had lives of our own, which did not help her much.

After advice from a consultant psychiatrist, who also happened to be of Asian origin, Mum left the United Kingdom and went back to live in Lahore in Pakistan. There, Dad had set up a large factory to make plastic bags for Pakistan's army. This business was very successful, and over time, I am led to believe, he became a 'rupee millionaire'.

I did not see Mum again and only heard from my elder brother, who managed to visit her in Lahore, that whilst Mum was not quite normal, she was much better and more comfortable back in Pakistan than she'd been in Glasgow.

CHAPTER 2

Growing Up in Glasgow

On arriving in Glasgow, we, as young children, had to start school almost immediately. I recall my first day walking to a local primary school with my two brothers. We were obviously excited to be going to school again. Our youngest brother was not old enough to start primary school at the same time as us. This would have been around September 1957. We were the only Asian pupils attending the school and, probably, the first Asian boys most, if not all, of the pupils at the school had ever seen.

On my first day at our new primary school, during the morning break, something happened that I found to be extremely distressing. All I can recall is simply standing with my two brothers in the middle of the playground with the rest of the school children, perhaps about 200, running around us for the whole break, shouting, laughing, and abusing us. I could not wait for the bell to sound so that we could return to our classes and escape this nightmare.

It was, for me, the most horrendous of experiences. The three of us said nothing to each other. We just stood still, terrified. No teacher came out to assist either. It was perhaps a bit like the cowboys marching round the Indians for a change! I have never forgotten that experience of my first day at a local Scottish primary school. It was so different from the experience of attending school in Pakistan. I am glad to say this did not happen again, and over time, we were accepted as part of the pupils of the school.

As time went on, I noticed how differently I was being treated by the other pupils. For example, when playing games that required two teams to be chosen by the boys, I was not valued in any way. I saw that, no matter the circumstances, I was unfairly treated and was always the last person to be chosen to join any team! My physical skills, which were very reasonable, were not considered at all. Also, I recall the occasions when we were taught how to do Scottish country dancing. I found that most of the girls did not want to be my dancing partner and would do everything they could to avoid being so. On one occasion when, as part of the dance two boys and two girls had to hold hands, my girl partner looked horrified and would not touch my brown hand.

I often wondered why this was the case, though I did not mention this to anyone. I did not know enough spoken English to do so and had no friend to discuss this with in any case. I simply had to take what was given and "go with the flow".

On another occasion when the boys had to take a shower following exercise, I found myself at the centre of laughter and derision. All the boys would come over to have a look at my "private part". This was because, as a Muslim child, I had been circumcised whilst they had not. I, therefore, looked different.

Because of these kinds of experiences as a child, I began to feel, for the first time in my life, that I did not belong here and was merely a foreigner and a stranger in this world. This feeling of "not belonging", despite living in Scotland for over sixty years, has never completely left me!

Education was important to our parents, this being the main reason for the family immigrating to Scotland in the first place. I was fortunate enough to have a very understanding and good primary school teacher, who helped me to catch up with the other pupils despite my having no English language to begin with. I was able to pick up the English language reasonably quickly, partly due to reading numerous Superman and other comics.

At the end of primary schooling, I did well enough to be allowed to progress on to a "senior secondary school" for further education. Later, my two younger brothers also achieved the same goal.

My elder brother, who was a year or so older than me, did not do well enough in school and was destined to go to a "junior secondary school" instead, with no chance of progressing on to a university education. He was as bright and gifted as the rest of us but was simply beaten by being just that little bit older and not acquiring the English language soon enough to a reasonable level to allow him to access a "senior secondary school" place. He, later, with help from Dad, went on to open a shop and make a living through business.

I am pleased to say that not everything was bad all the time. I do remember one incident that took place at the last school assembly before my class moved on to secondary school. The headmistress spoke to all the schoolchildren and told us all that this would be the last time my class would be at the school assembly. She wished our class all the very best in the future.

She then told the school that she had a specific question to ask us all. My class had completed a very difficult test in English grammar, which she had just finished marking. This test was so difficult that only one person had managed to give all the correct answers. She asked the schoolchildren if anyone could guess who that person in our class might be. Several hands shot up, and various names were mentioned. However, none of these were correct. Finally, before dismissing the assembly, the headmistress said, to my utter surprise, that the only person who had got all the questions right was Riaz. And she was sure I would do well in the future! No one said anything to me about the headmistress's statement, but it was, nevertheless, a very good and encouraging way for me to begin my further studies at secondary school.

As far as religious education is concerned, both our parents were keen for us to learn more about Islam. They were both Muslims and followed the teachings of the Koran. They wanted all their children to do the same. We were thus encouraged to attend a Koran learning school situated on the South Side of the River Clyde in Glasgow. It was a room in a tenement building at that time, though there is beautiful mosque there now.

I am not sure that we gained a great deal from attending this Koran learning class. All that seemed to happen was that the teacher would say a phrase of the Koran in Arabic, and we simply had to repeat it. If we did not do well enough to repeat what he said, he would not hesitate to hit

13

our hand with a ruler! There was no attempt to teach the meaning of what was being learnt. It was only necessary to learn the Arabic words by rote. The class was not well run, and after attending for about a year or so, we all decided to stop going.

Our religious learning input would come primarily from Mum, as Dad was away from home for much of the time. She taught us to respect other faiths but to remember that Islam was the last, final, and full word from Allah through the Prophet Muhammad.

There obviously was an arrangement for Mum to have some income made available to her so that she could look after herself and her four sons whilst Dad was away much of the time. Unfortunately, this was never enough, and consequently we often did not have enough money to buy food to last the whole week. So, we frequently went hungry, especially at weekends. I did not, of course, tell anyone of this situation. I was too ashamed to do so; besides, there were many other people in the world who were even worse off than I was.

I also recall during my time at secondary school that I did not have enough money to pay for school dinners. The other problem was that, as a Muslim, I would not be allowed to eat any meat at the school dinners anyway. This was because the meat would not be considered "halal" (meat from animals that have been slaughtered in the prescribed way in accordance with the Sharia Islamic law). I, therefore, walked home every day at lunchtime, and with the money I did have to spend, I bought a small tin of beans and a small tin of rice. This was my lunch every day of the school week. No wonder I was very thin then!

I recall once seeing something on the television that disturbed me greatly when I was about fourteen years of age. There was some indication from the media that China may have acquired the atomic bomb. For some reason, I began to think that there may be a world war again and was deeply concerned about what would happen in the future. I began to ask myself all kinds of questions. Would we all be killed? What happens when we die? Is there life after death? What is religion all about?

One question—which religion was the correct one?—seemed to stick in my mind. Was it, as I had been told by my parents, Islam? Or were there some other forms of worship that would also be acceptable to God? Would God accept all religions? Did God even exist?

With these thoughts in mind, I recall saying a prayer to God one night, looking for answers to this dilemma. My prayer was not "theologically correct," so to speak, but it was said quite sincerely. I believe God heard my prayer and graciously answered it in His own way and in His own time!

The prayer, I said, went something like this: "Dear God, if there is a God, and you are interested in me—I don't know why you would be interested in a foreigner such as me; no one else is—but if you are there and show yourself to me, I will follow you."

I suppose part of the reason for me thinking about religion may have been related to my joining the Boys' Brigade a few years earlier. A local Church of Scotland minister had come to my primary school just as we were about to leave for secondary schooling and had invited all the boys to join the Boys' Brigade company he was associated with. I was very eager to do so, particularly as it would mean that I could play football and take part in other physical activities with boys of my own age. I was also hoping to make friends with some of the boys, as I had no real friend and found life to be very lonely. I asked Mum if I could join the Boys' Brigade and was told that that would not be a problem.

As I grew up in the Boys' Brigade, I began to learn something about the teachings of the Bible. After all, the objective of the Boys Brigade is "the advancement of Christ's kingdom among boys and the promotion of habits of obedience, reverence, discipline, self-respect, and all that tends towards a true Christian manliness". I learnt that people who followed Jesus were called "Christians". Unlike Muslims, who would worship Allah on a Friday, they went to church on a Sunday to worship God there.

As time went on, I began to learn more about how the Christian boys in the Boys' Brigade lived. I sadly, from my own perspective, found the type of lives these Christian boys lived was not very attractive and certainly not what I would call "holy".

I discovered that many of them, though too young, began to smoke and drink alcohol. They were often insolent to the officers who gave their time voluntarily to assist in the Boys' Brigade. Sadly, they were not good examples of what being a Christian should be. I, at that time, of course, had no idea of the difference between a true Christian believer and a nominal Christian. I was led to believe that everyone who was born in a

Christian country, such as the United Kingdom, was a Christian, except someone like me.

Even though I attended the Boys' Brigade regularly and, over time, won several prizes and was finally appointed to the position of staff sergeant, I did not feel I was given much respect by the other boys. I suspect this was due to the colour of my skin more than anything else. I was a foreigner, and no matter what, I did not really belong here!

I cannot forget one incident that was particularly difficult for me to come to terms with. I was part of our Boys' Brigade football team and loved playing football. On one Saturday morning, I turned up to play a game of football against another Boys' Brigade team, as arranged on the previous Friday as usual. When I was getting ready and changing into my football gear to play, it transpired that another boy, not known to me, came into our changing room. He came just to greet some of his friends on our team. He was a member of a neighbouring Boys' Brigade company. He was apparently well known to several of the other boys, who were also changing to play football.

I heard some conversations taking place but was not fully aware of what was happening. As I was ready to play and go out onto the field, the officer in charge of the football team approached me to say that he had some news for me. Then, to my utter astonishment, he told me he had found another person to play in my place and that I was dropped from the team. I was deeply disappointed, especially as I knew that the boy who would be taking my place was not part of our Boys' Brigade company and, therefore, in my view, could not play for our team, as he was ineligible to do so. I was told by the officer in charge of the team that all the other boys knew that this boy was a good footballer, and the team would have a better chance of winning if he was on the team. So, I was to say nothing and simply accept the situation.

I left for home as the game began. I was very disappointed and did not play for the team again. It was not, in my view, a good example of fair and decent behaviour. It made me feel, even more strongly, that I was not one of the boys. I was a stranger and a foreigner, and no one cared for me.

As it so happened, the company finally folded totally unexpectedly. It was due to one of the boys stealing the captain's gloves. The captain lined up all the boys and asked that his gloves be returned. The person or persons who had taken the gloves refused to own up or give them back. The boys did not take the captain seriously. They began to joke about the theft, accusing one another of being the thief. I was also accused of taking the gloves.

The captain gave a clear and serious warning that, if his gloves were not returned immediately, the company would be dissolved that night. Despite his very severe warning, no one owned up! So, that was the end of the company and, at the same time, the end of my career in the Boys' Brigade.

Still, I learned one very important thing from this sad experience—as I had been taught at home, Islam was a better religion than any other! For example, I did not smoke or drink alcohol. Nor was I ever insolent to my senior officers. I respected them all and was extremely grateful too for the time and effort they gave voluntarily to us boys.

I would never, ever have considered stealing my captain's gloves. Why would anyone do such a thing and then not own up? If this was how Christians behaved, the Christian religion was clearly inferior to Islam and certainly not for me!

CHAPTER 3

School Dux Medal and Publicity

hilst coming to the end of my involvement in the Boys' Brigade, I was also coming to the end of my fourth and final year at my secondary school. It was a difficult time, as the future seemed somewhat uncertain. Then some totally unexpected publicity came my way.

I had gained the highest overall marks in the school among the boys on my school examinations. As was the custom at that time, I was awarded the boys' "Dux Medal" for being first in my year. In addition, I was also fortunate enough to win the top prize for science studies, and the teaching staff had voted for me to be appointed vice captain of the school.

I did gain the information that some of the teachers would have been happy for me to be appointed captain of the school, but for a coloured boy to be given that appointment in 1966 was perhaps a step too far. It so happened that one of the boys in my class, whom I met at secondary school, had become a very close friend. He was the one who was appointed captain of the school. As he was second to me in the examination results, I was content with the outcome.

One day, following the announcement of the examination results, I was approached by the school headmaster, as he wanted to speak to me about something important. I had no idea what he wanted. Totally to me surprise, he asked me if it would be permissible for him to let a local newspaper know of my achievements at the school. His view was that it would be very good publicity for the school should that happen.

After all, I was an immigrant in the country. But, despite this fact, it was obvious that I had been given opportunity to learn and progress. I was not only the boys' dux medallist with the top science prize; I was also vice captain of the school and had been appointed staff sergeant in a local Boys' Brigade company. It seemed clear to him that many of my accomplishments would have been denied me in many other countries and other circumstances.

Having discussed this with my parents, and with their agreement, I was content for the local newspaper to be given the information. I took the view that receiving some publicity would be a good thing for the school. As I was about to leave the school to go to another, this was at least something useful I could do before my final departure.

I do not think that the headmaster, or indeed anyone, could have guessed what would happen following the release of my "success story" to the local newspaper.

No sooner had the headmaster gotten in touch with a local newspaper, than I found myself harassed by several reporters knocking at my home door looking for more information for their newspaper articles. The next thing that happened was that I was invited to be interviewed on television, and my story was broadcast to the nation in the evening news. If that was not enough, this was followed by my being interviewed on radio. Unknown to me, the radio interview was then broadcast to all the Commonwealth countries throughout the world! There was no way that anyone could have predicted that this would happen.

Following all this unexpected publicity, I received a letter from my maternal grandfather, who was headmaster in Lahore. It turned out that, just by chance, he was listening to the English news on the radio and heard me being interviewed. He could not believe what he was hearing. He immediately wrote to me in English to let me know how proud he was of his grandson and that, in his view, I was a great 'Son of Pakistan'. This was the one and only direct communication I had from my grandfather; sadly, he passed away soon after this time.

Due to this experience in my life, I became even more conscious of the way people behaved towards me and what they wanted from me. I discovered during my interviews with the reporters that, whilst they certainly were very keen to speak to me, this was only to get information for their newspaper articles. They were not interested in me as a person at all.

To make things even worse, some information about me that appeared in the newspapers was not accurate but was published anyway. For example, I had taken seven O level examinations and, like everyone else in the country, was awaiting the results. Despite my saying on several occasions that the result of the O level examinations was "not yet known", the newspapers still published that I had "passed" all seven O level examinations. Consequently, some people criticised me for saying that I had passed my examinations, when the results were not yet known. Many refused to believe me when I said that I had not given this wrong information to the reporters.

Fortunately, some weeks later when the results were officially announced, it was the case that I had managed to pass all seven examinations. Despite that, the experience made me believe that the reporters were only interested in writing a story for their own purposes. None of them were at all that interested in me. I suppose being a foreigner and a stranger in this world makes you very sensitive to these things!

CHAPTER 4

Journey of Faith Begins

hilst I may have forgotten the "prayer" I had said a few years earlier to God, asking Him to reveal himself to me so that I could follow Him, graciously God had not forgotten it.

After all the unexpected publicity had died down, I went on a two-week holiday camp run by the school. This took place in July 1966. Now that I look back to that time, I think Mum must have made a great financial sacrifice for me to be able to do this. Perhaps this was her way of rewarding me for my achievements; sadly, though, I did not think much about it at the time. I was very keen to go on this school camp simply because my school friend and others wanted to do so, and it was something exciting to do during the summer holidays. How I wish now that I had taken the time to thank Mum for her kindness to me despite our lack of financial resources.

The holiday camp was held in a school called Golspie High School, which is situated on the north-east coast of Scotland. This holiday time would be my last contact with the school. After the summer holidays, I would be moving on to study for "higher examinations" at another senior secondary school in Glasgow called Whitehill Secondary School.

I had to change schools because at the time I attended John Street Secondary School, it only taught up to fourth year. Those pupils who were considered able could sit O level examinations before finishing secondary schooling. Many pupils could leave school even after third year without sitting O level examinations at all.

Those pupils who wished to go onto study at a university needed to pass enough "higher" examinations to allow entrance. As I wished to study medicine at a university, I needed to continue my studies at this other non-fee-paying local school in order to gain "higher" qualifications to allow entry into a university.

On arrival at the school holiday camp, we met up with a former pupil of the school who was part of the leadership team. He was by this time an art student and must have been in his early twenties. I noticed that he tended to wear his college scarf round his neck much of the time. I was impressed by that, as I wanted to be a student too. We learnt that, for some years, he had spent his holiday from college helping at this school camp. He did this at his own expense, utilising his own free time to do so. I was, of course, totally unaware of this, till I met him at the holiday camp.

When he was asked why he chose to help at the school camp like he did, his answer was very surprising to me. He told us that he did this because he was led to believe this was God's will for him at this time in his life. However, this would be his last visit to the camp because of his evolving life circumstances. On this last occasion, he would spend the first week of his holiday time with the school camp but would then move on to spend his second week at a Christian seaside mission camp. From then on, he would assist at the other camp, whilst still an art student.

As I observed this young man's behaviour, I discovered that he was somehow different from any other person I had ever met before. He had a definite personal relationship with God. He, as it were, "walked with God". And somehow, I knew, "God walked with him!" He told me that he was a "born-again Christian" and followed Jesus Christ. This, of course, did not mean much to me, as I had little knowledge of Christian theology. I could, however, see quite clearly that he had a genuine loving and courteous attitude towards everyone he met, which included me as well! This meant a great deal to me, as I had not come across this before.

We did not have great conversations about religion and, certainly, had no arguments about Islam and Christianity. He simply lived out his life of love in the service of his master Jesus Christ, doing whatever was required of him. The way he treated me showed clearly that he did not see me only as a foreigner and a coloured person of little worth. Instead, he just saw me as a valued and beloved person, a friend, and even a child of God. This contrasted completely with the way some of the school pupils treated me. Many of them made fun of me behind my back and even called me names, though usually when they thought I could not hear them! This was probably because they knew that they would be smacked if I heard them say discourteous things about me in my hearing. I was quite big and a strong lad by this time.

I was overcome when, on his departure, after one week of the holiday camp, he told me he would be praying for me. I could not work out why he would take time and effort to pray for me. He did not owe me anything. I had never been in his company before, and yet he was prepared to pray for a foreigner and a stranger such as me. No one had ever told me that they would pray for me before. I knew he meant what he said!

CHAPTER 5

An Experience with God

During the second week of the school holiday camp, after the art student had left, something totally unexpected happened. I had had a very difficult, tiring, and depressing day. But for some reason, I woke up in the middle of the night out of my sleep. As soon as I did so, I realised immediately that I was in the presence of the living God. I did not hear anything or see any visible sign or any such thing. But somehow, I just knew God was there in the room with me. I broke down in tears!

God was utterly holy, and I was sinful, helpless, hopeless, and useless. How I wished the ground would, somehow, open and swallow me and hide me from His holy presence. I had no excuse to offer to God for my useless life. There was no thought of me being a good Muslim or even a good person. There was no thought concerning my never swearing, or not smoking or not drinking alcohol. No! I was simply a hopeless, sinful person trying to somehow hide from the presence of a Holy God!

Then, and I still do not know how to this day, I knew that the presence of the living God in that room with me was none other than Jesus Christ! It was not an angel or Abraham or Moses, prophets of God I knew about from the Koran. It was not the Muslim Prophet Muhammad. No, it was the Lord Jesus Christ!

Then I discovered, to my utter surprise, that Jesus was not condemning me at all. No, I was simply condemning myself! There was no doubt whatsoever that, on my own merit, I could never face Him. I was lost and helpless. What could I do?

At that point, whilst I don't think I heard a physical voice I, nevertheless, heard Jesus say in my mind, *Riaz, come follow me*. At the same time, I saw him wave his hand of invitation, which I could not refuse.

The whole experience felt as though I was just a poor beggar sitting in the dirt of the ground where I belonged, being ignored by all. Then who should come along but the Prince of Glory Himself, riding on a magnificent white horse? To my utter surprise, He stops where I am and puts out His hand to pull me up behind him to take me to His home!

I remember at this point saying a prayer that Christians often use but that no one had ever taught me. I said simply, "Come into my heart, Lord Jesus. I can't live without you. From this day on, I will follow you." That night, I became a Christian! I knew nothing about the theology of Christianity. But I knew one thing—Jesus was my friend and saviour. I could not live without Him. From now on, I would follow only Him.

I did not tell anyone of this experience. I simply kept it to myself and thought about it. What did all this mean? Then, as the weeks and months went past, I began to hear a voice in my mind saying, *Read the Bible, Riaz. Read the Bible*. But how could I read the Bible? In a Muslim home, there would certainly be a copy of the Koran, kept at the highest point in the home, but not a copy of the Bible.

Then I remembered. Yes! There was a Bible in my home. Some people, known as the Gideons, had come to my school three years earlier and had given everyone at the school assembly a copy of the New Testament and Psalms for free. I had taken a book home, like everyone else, but had never actually read it.

I looked for this book and found it. I then began to read it. I read it for hours at a time! I read:

> For God so loved the world, that he gave his only begotten
> Son, that whosoever believeth in him should not perish,
> but have everlasting life. For God sent not his Son into the
> world to condemn the world; but that the world through
> him might be saved. (John 3:16–17, KJV)

By this time, I had been living in Glasgow for over ten years, but no one had ever told me that God loved me! I had never heard that message being read from the Koran either.

As I read further, I could not believe what was written in the Bible about Jesus. He was tried, and, despite there being no evidence against him, He was crucified by the Roman soldiers! He had done no wrong. I found it difficult to comprehend how human beings could possibly do such a dreadful thing to such a wonderful person as Jesus. To my complete surprise, I read Jesus praying whilst on the cross:

> Then said Jesus, "Father, forgive them; for they know not what they do." (Luke 23:34, KJV)

How could He pray for the forgiveness of his enemies? They did not deserve that. They were making fun of Him even as He was dying on the Cross. I read on and found the angel saying:

> And as they were afraid, and bowed down their faces to the earth, they said unto them, "Why seek ye the living among the dead? He is not here but is risen." (Luke 24:5–6, KJV)

I was overcome with wonder and joy. He had come back to life. Jesus was alive! Of course, He must have been alive. I had met Him at Golspie High School! I met him again through reading the bible.

As time went on, I began to meet up with other lads who were Christians. This included my friend from school. He apparently had also been influenced by the art student at the holiday camp and was encouraged to make more of his faith. He told me that he had decided some years earlier, whilst attending a local church, to follow Jesus but had never shared that with anyone till now.

I then began to think about attending a church to worship Jesus with other believers. But where did one go? I had no idea of where the churches were and what they stood for. I had attended a church on an occasion through the Boys' Brigade, but that church was too big and too far away for me.

Then one Saturday evening, as I was standing with a friend sheltering from the rain in the entrance of a tenement in London Road, a man came along the road in obvious distress. I immediately felt sorry for him and wanted to speak to him to see why he was so upset. My friend warned me not to approach the man, thinking he must be under the influence of alcohol. However, I did go forward and asked him why he was so upset.

At this he looked at me and, to my surprise, said, "I have lost my Bible."

I was immediately sympathetic, as the Bible had become very important to me. I asked him, "Where is it?"

He replied, "Down the road."

I asked him, "Why don't you go and get it?"

To this, he replied that the door of the building was closed and would not open till next Wednesday at 7.30 p.m.

"Why don't you go back and get your Bible then?" I asked.

To this question, he replied, "I am afraid." Then he looked at me and asked, "Will you come with me?"

I said that I would be happy to do so on the coming Wednesday and would meet him outside the building. He then went on his way quite contented.

I went to the said building on the next Wednesday evening, as agreed, but did not see the man I'd met earlier. I saw several young people going into the building and soon heard music and singing about Jesus. I wondered if he was perhaps inside the building already, and I may have just missed him going in. So, I went in to see if he was there. As I reached the top of the stairs, I had to sit down on the nearest available empty chair, as an older man stood up to speak. Very soon I realised that this man was speaking about the same Jesus I knew!

I did not see the man who said he had lost his Bible in the building that night. No one knew anything about him, and I never met him again. But in God's providence, I had found a place for fellowship and worship. This place was known locally as the 428 Club, as the building's address was 428 London Road. Here, various church members met every Wednesday night to sing Christian songs and preach the gospel message to the young people in the deprived area of Bridgeton. This became my "church" for some time, through which I learnt a great deal more about Jesus.

Who was the man who told me he had lost his Bible at the 428 Club? I don't know. It has been suggested by some that he might have been an angel! Whatever the truth, I could not have continued my Christian journey in a better way than by attending the prayer meeting and the outreach to the young people of Bridgeton through the 428 Club. It was just what I needed. I attended regularly every week for years and met many people, some of whom became lifelong friends, including a girl called Janet, who was to become my wife.

CHAPTER 6

Witnessing to the Family

Encouraged by the teaching at the 428 Club, my school friend and I began attending open-air meetings for witnessing to others about Jesus. This tended to be in the city centre of Glasgow, usually on a Saturday night.

Whilst I was telling friends and people passing by in Sauchiehall Street in Glasgow city centre about my new-found faith in Jesus, I had not yet told my own family!

I have discovered over the years that, when you have to get over a spiritual hurdle that is just too high for you, the good Lord Jesus does not abandon you to it, demanding that you get over it all by yourself. Instead, rather graciously, he helps you overcome the hurdle. He even carries you over it Himself if need be! This is what He did for me, as I just could not bring myself round to tell my family about my new-found Christian faith.

One evening on coming home, I was informed by a young cousin that my father wanted to speak to me on my own. My father would not normally ever speak to me in such a way! So, I knew something extremely unusual was happening. I think that someone in the Muslim community must have heard me speaking about Jesus in the city centre, and the word had gotten back to the family about me doing so, causing extreme alarm for everyone.

When I went into the room to speak to my father, he was clearly upset. He was standing in the middle of the room. As I entered the room, he looked at me and asked in a very serious tone, "What's this I hear about you? Are you a Christian?"

I had no choice. I had to answer that question honestly. Three of the hardest words I have ever had to say in my entire life were, "Yes, I am." These words were not said with great conviction and power but in a very timid and weak way!

However, my father must have accepted my answer as being genuine. As a result of my answer to his question, he virtually never really spoke to me again. I was no longer one of his sons.

I am not altogether sure why I was not thrown out of our home. I am guessing that it might have been the influence of my mother, who may have insisted that it was not appropriate for this to happen. After all, I was by this time quite well known in the community, given the publicity that I had received. Some may have thought that it was not honourable for the Muslim community to have one of their own boys living on the streets!

Things did, however, change radically for me, even though I was still living in the family home. I ended up staying in an attic room by myself, eating alone and doing my own things. If my father happened to come up the stairs and I was going down the stairs, he would simply look the other way. He no longer showed any interest in my life.

A few weeks after telling my father about having become a Christian, I received a totally unexpected visit from some men. The people who came to see me had apparently been invited by my father to speak to me about religious issues. They were two older men who were recognised Muslim scholars from London. They shook my hand and tried to start a conversation about the correctness of Muslim theology. They were accompanied by a young man who, at the start of the discussion, made it clear that he did not know anything about Christianity. As I started to tell him some basic facts about Christianity, the senior person interrupted the conversation and said that was the end of their visit, after which they all got up and left.

Sometime later, to my surprise, my father asked if I would be agreeable to having an organised debate concerning the spiritual issues raised in Islam and Christianity. The arguments, from the Christian side, would be presented by the pastor who spoke regularly at the 428 Club. He would be up against one of the leaders of the mosque in Glasgow, who would present the Islamic point of view.

I agreed that it would be good to discuss matters further but took the view that every person listening to the debate should be free to make up his or her own mind as to what was the truth. This did not go down at all well with my father. He was certain that the Christians would lose the debate but, despite that, would continue to believe what was not true. Hence, he concluded there was no point in going to the trouble of organising a debate about my new-found faith. The matter thus ended without any debate taking place.

Thereafter, there was no real contact between my family and me for several years. Even my elder brother said that I had gone mad. However, on one and only one occasion, my mother did acknowledge my new-found faith by telling me something I did not know anything about.

She was doing some housework when I happened to come into the room. She looked up at me and simply said, "It must be in the genes!"

I, of course, did not know what she meant and so asked her for the meaning of her statement. She went on to explain that her father, my grandfather, had a similar religious experience. He was apparently born into and brought up in a high-class Hindu family in India who believed in many gods. When he heard, through the teaching of Islam, that there was only one God and he alone should be worshipped, my grandfather immediately announced to the family that he was no longer a Hindu but would from now on follow the one God, Allah. He became a committed Muslim.

Soon thereafter, India split into different countries. Muslims set up an Islamic country known as West Pakistan and East Pakistan. These two parts of Pakistan were miles apart, with India in between, but they were considered one country. Many Muslims left various parts of India and became citizens of the new Muslim country. My grandfather, so Mum told me, gave up everything he had to follow the "people of God" into West Pakistan, to start a new religious life. He remained a committed Muslim for the rest of his life and brought up his family in the Muslim tradition.

I was spellbound to hear this story and had never previously been aware of it. I did wonder, with some sadness, if my grandfather had ever heard the Christian gospel and had heard about Jesus, would he have left everything and followed Him? This was the only religious conversation

I ever had with my mother following my conversion to Christianity. I wondered if it was because of her father's experience that she was quietly supportive of me, though she never gave up following Islam herself.

On one other occasion, my uncle from my mother's side came to speak to me. He was an educated person who had attended university back in Pakistan. He had also come to live in the United Kingdom, though he went back to Pakistan regularly. He started off by telling me that he was an experienced and well-travelled person and understood the different things people believed.

He then told me that my father had said to him that, if I were to say that I was no longer a Christian and revert back to Islam, he would buy me a car to take me to Glasgow University and give me a gift of £1,000. He then suggested that we were both "men of the world", and I did not need to believe anything or could believe whatever I wanted. However, it was in my best interest to simply say to my father that I was a Muslim after all. The reward I would gain would be well worth it.

On hearing this suggestion, I said, "I am sorry, Uncle, but why are you trying to corrupt me? I follow Jesus and will continue to do so no matter what the cost!"

This ended the conversation, and I did not hear from my uncle again.

The very next day, I was, as usual, standing at a bus stop waiting to catch a bus to go to Glasgow University from Bridgeton. But no bus came! I was worried about being late for class. It was raining very heavily, and I was soaking wet. A car would have been very handy indeed! Just at that moment, my father's sister came along the road. I turned around to greet her, only to see my aunt looking at me as though I was covered in dog's dirt and then walk on, looking the other way. Boy was I glad that it was raining very heavily that day! It hid my tears, so no passers-by would see me crying!

The number 64 bus did eventually arrive, and I made my way to the university. That day I really felt, more than ever, that I was an unwanted stranger and did not belong anywhere.

The relationship, particularly with my father, was never restored. He was away on business much of the time in any case, and I did not see him again for many years. Later, he did give his time and effort to arrange important things such as Muslim marriage arrangements for my three brothers. Two of these took place in Pakistan. Hence, there was no possibility for me to attend, though there was no invitation in any case. However, when my youngest brother got married, the Muslim wedding took place in Birmingham. To my surprise, and great delight, my family was invited to this wedding, and we attended as a family. By this time, I had two children, who would have been around nine and eleven years of age.

Things were not perfect. Nevertheless, we all seemed to have a good time at my brother's wedding. I was given the privilege of sitting with the groom, as one of his brothers, on a stage in front of the whole congregation. When prayers were said, my Muslim brothers lifted their arms in prayer, whilst I closed my eyes and bent my head in prayer to the Lord. No one seemed to object. Then, as was the custom, my father and the bride's father left the room to speak to the bride for her consent to the marriage. She was not present in the hall with others but was waiting for her father next door! The rest of the day also went well, and we returned home quite satisfied, having been able to attend the wonderful occasion of my youngest brother's Muslim wedding.

It was not till many years later that I discovered the pain and sadness that was felt by my nine-year-old daughter at her uncle's wedding. She chose not to tell me anything about what had happened at the wedding till she was much older. This was to prevent my heartbreak. Despite her young age, she was obviously very wise and cared about her dad's feelings. The circumstances were quite simple. She was looking forward to the wedding of her uncle, whom she did not know well. But, even more so, she was excited to meet her other granddad for the very first time.

By this time, she had had a very good and close relationship with her maternal grandparents and thought that it would be just as good to meet her grandparents from my side of the family as well. She did not see her grandmother because, as it so happened, she was not at the wedding. She was not very well and, by this time, had gone back to Pakistan to live in Lahore. She, apparently, was not fit enough to come to the wedding. Furthermore, my father was accompanied by his "other" wife, as he had two wives by this time. This was allowed under Islamic law in Pakistan.

As expected, my daughter saw my father in my brother's house. She was devastated to discover that her granddad was not interested in her or her elder brother. He refused to speak to either of them. It seemed to her that, in his eyes, she did not exist. She found that, at her young age, to be a very painful experience. But to protect me, she did not tell me about her feelings till years later! What a wonderful daughter God has given me!

Despite being at a family wedding and seeing my father, I found there was very little real contact between my father and me. I suppose his having another wife in the place of my mother accompanying him did not make things any easier. Nevertheless, it was great to be at a family wedding for the very first time.

It was not till many more years had passed that there seemed to be just a little change for the better. I got a phone call from my elder brother telling me that Dad was not well and had been taken to hospital in Germany! He had severe jaundice due to gallstones and was awaiting a major operation. Dad was not sure whether to give permission for the German consultant to go ahead with the operation. He wanted me to speak to the consultant and discuss matters with him and then advise if the operation should go ahead. By this time, I was a consultant surgeon myself, and he wanted my input into an important decision concerning a possible life- threatening operation.

I was able to speak to the consultant in Germany over the phone. Fortunately, his English was excellent. I discussed my father's clinical condition with him. It was clear that one of the gallstones was obstructing the common bile duct, which clearly needed to be explored and the gallstone removed.

I agreed with the consultant surgeon that the operation should go ahead and was content for him to proceed as he had planned. I heard later from my elder brother that the operation was done successfully, and that Dad made a good recovery. There was no direct communication with Dad. Still I was pleased that I could play a little part in bringing him back to good health.

Meanwhile, Mum's medical condition deteriorated further. Sadly, I heard that she had died in Pakistan. Under Islamic tradition, she was buried before the sun went down, so there was no possibility of my being able to attend her funeral. May she rest in peace.

Some years later, I heard that Dad and his second wife were now retired from work in Pakistan and that they were living in Huddersfield in England. I believe that this was to allow his second wife to be closer to her relatives, who also lived in Huddersfield.

There was no contact directly between us until, once again, I received information from my elder brother that Dad was again seriously ill. He had developed terminal leukaemia, and there was nothing more that could be done for him. He was preparing to depart this world. My brother indicated that my father was keen to see me before he died.

My wife, Janet, and I drove down to the hospital to see him. When we arrived, he was feeling reasonably well. We were able to spend an hour or so with him. We spent most of the time just sharing work and family news. I was told that Dad had not been informed about the fact that I had developed a hepatitis B infection and its consequences so that he would not be upset, given his terminal condition. I, therefore, did not raise the matter.

At the end of our conversation, he looked at me and told me that he now lived across the road from the mosque. He also told me that he spent more time in the mosque than in his house. Furthermore, he said that he spent much of his time praying for the family. He then turned around and said that he prayed for me as well!

This was the last time I saw my father. I received a phone call at home some days later from my elder brother, informing me that my father had passed away. He wondered if I wanted to come to the funeral, which would take place that same day. I decided that, if I did go, I would simply get in the way of the Muslim funeral and it was perhaps best to leave it be. Sad as it was, I was glad that I had the opportunity of speaking to my father before he left this world. May he also rest in peace.

Perhaps because of these sad experiences, partly shared with my elder brother, there was a bond formed between us—with the result that we began to meet up from time to time. This usually meant that we would go to his house for a meal and general family talk. This still continues. However, it is the case that "religious" matters are not openly discussed. He continues to follow the Muslim faith. Having raised much capital to help build a local mosque where he lives, he serves as one of the leaders there. What the future holds, only God knows.

CHAPTER 7

Life as a Medical Student

One of the most privileged experiences I have had in my life has been the opportunity to study medicine at Glasgow University. I could not have been happier and more grateful to God on receiving the letter from Glasgow University informing me of my successful application to study medicine there. Whilst I would have been content to study medicine at any university, from a practical point of view, living and studying in Glasgow was the most manageable for my situation.

It was not at all easy achieving adequate entry qualifications for university. I had to change schools to study for the higher examinations, as the secondary school I attended only went up to the lower O levels standard. I was not the only pupil in this situation. A dozen other pupils from my school had to do the same in order to gain entrance to university.

It turned out that we were all so far behind in our studies compared with the pupils who had always been at this school that all but me and two others from my former school left after only a few weeks. They all took the view that there was no point continuing further study at the school, as we were so far behind that passing higher examinations would not be possible. All thought that gaining some sort of paid employment was a far better option for them. I had no other option but to continue studying in the hope that I would somehow manage to catch up and do enough to get into university.

As we were so far behind the other pupils, particularly in science subjects, my friend and I were told by the teacher in charge of teaching science subjects that there was nothing he could do for us. He had to concentrate in teaching his regular pupils, as that was where his priority lay. We would have to just sit in the class whilst the other pupils continued their studies uninterrupted. We were on our own! This was not very encouraging.

It soon became clear that, whilst we were far behind the others in chemistry and physics, fortunately, we were not too far behind in English, maths, and geography. As I wished to study medicine, I had no choice. I had to somehow catch up in the science subjects, as this was essential for gaining entry to a suitable university course. It was also obvious that I would have to study for the next two years and would only then have any chance of gaining entry into university.

I studied as hard as I could, using the science books that were available to me. As expected, there was no input from any teacher. At the end of the year, I sat the higher science examination, passing only with a C grade. I was a little disappointed, as I was hoping to have done better.

When the results came out, my science teacher at one point said that he could not believe I had passed my science higher. He thought that I must have been very lucky with the questions asked in the examination. He had not expected either me or my friend from John Street School, who was the runner up to me for the dux of the year award, to do anything other than fail. Sadly, he was right as far as my friend was concerned.

When in the following year, after having studied further on my own, I also managed a pass in higher chemistry and higher physics as separate subjects, the teacher was speechless! He could not believe I had managed passes in these two subjects. He had not thought that this was possible.

I managed enough passes in all the other higher examination subjects to gain entry into Glasgow University to study medicine. I am most grateful to God and can't help but thank Him for helping me get through this extremely difficult time.

When I started my studies at Glasgow University, I had to get to the university by bus, as I had no other means of transport. It did mean going on a number 64 bus from the east end of the city, through the city centre and to the west end of the city, where the University of Glasgow was situated. It was a long and tedious journey.

On my very first day as I was about to go to the university, Mum approached me and said that she had something to give me to take to the university. Her gift turned out to be a beautiful and expensive-looking leather bag, in which I could carry my medical books. She must have gone to the Glasgow city centre shops herself and bought it for me. She must have sacrificed a lot to do this. I suspect this was a family tradition that she remembered from her younger days, when her brothers went to university for the first time back home in Pakistan. Despite knowing about my Christian faith, she still chose to give me this wonderful and useful gift. I would no longer need a plastic carrier bag for my books. I still have that bag to this day. It is the only family gift I possess. Thanks, Mum!

When my bus finally reached Glasgow University and I was about to get off the bus, quite unexpectedly, the bus driver spoke to me. I, of course, did not know him. He asked me if this was my first day at the university. I said quite proudly that it was. He then asked if I was going to study medicine.

I replied, "Yes that's right."

He then looked at me, smiled, and said, "Thought so. Good luck, son."

I think he must have recognised me from the media attention I'd had some two years before. What an encouraging way for a stranger and foreigner travelling from the poor Bridgeton area to the more affluent west of Glasgow to start the first day at university!

In those days, students were given a grant to help with the cost of living whilst studying full-time. The amount granted was dependent on the earnings and tax returns of the father of the student. This, of course, caused a major problem for me. My father was away on business much of the time and was not at all keen to fill in forms for my benefit—so much so that it became a serious issue. I didn't know from year to year how much of a grant I would receive, if any, and I was unsure as to whether I could continue my studies from one year to the next. This caused unnecessary stress during my years of study.

I shared this problem with the consultant who was assigned as a mentor to me as a first-year medical student. He was a consultant psychiatrist of Jewish origin! I had shared my testimony with him on an occasion previously when I and some other students were invited as guests to his home. As a consultant psychiatrist, he was fascinated by the experience I'd had with God at Golspie High School. He clearly did not know what to make of it. However, after he'd questioned me quite a lot on the subject, I did get the impression that he eventually concluded that I was not insane!

He advised me to write to the Glasgow University Board telling them of my difficulty due to my commitment to Jesus and asking if there was any way they could help me concerning the grant issue. I took his advice and wrote a brief letter to the board. I received a very nice reply telling me that the board had great sympathy for my situation but was not able to interfere or assist in any way. I was naturally sorry to read this response but was delighted that at least a part of my testimony had been recorded in the records of the Board of Glasgow University!

I am pleased to say that, though I could do nothing to overcome this problem, I did get a "provisional" grant each year. This meant that the amount of the grant available to me was not known and was only "finalised" when the relevant information came into the university from my father. My father did submit the relevant forms, though never on time. Perhaps, unknown to me, this was due to the influence of the family and Muslim community, who may have put some pressure on my father to do the necessary paperwork. Also, when my younger brother started university, he needed forms completed as well to receive an appropriate grant, and this would have been some benefit for me too. The problem went on year after year whilst I was a student. Finally, three months after I qualified as a doctor, I received a cheque from the university, advising me that I had been underpaid the year before! God is faithful!

The other problem I had to overcome as a student was to find a paid job during the summer holidays. The university course at that time lasted six years with a three-month break over the summer period. While the grant paid the university fees, getting paid employment during the summer holidays was essential in my situation, to allow me to buy books and clothes. But where would I get a summer job? I had no-one I could approach for advice, never mind knowing someone who would give me a job. So, all I could do was pray in earnest and ask the Good Lord for His help to find an appropriate job.

The next day, after praying about the matter, I was walking down the road when I saw a sign in a tailor's shop advertising a temporary post.

44

I thought, how excellent! This must be for me. I went into the shop and asked if I, as a medical student, could be considered for the post advertised in the window. The general manager was called and came out of his office to speak to me.

He took one look at me and simply said, "Sorry. That is a mistake. We should have taken that sign down, as the post is filled."

I went away a little discouraged. But not as discouraged as I was the following day when I saw that the sign was still there and had not been taken down. This showed me again that, despite everything, I was still a stranger and foreigner in this world.

The following day, I took a walk down High Street in Glasgow, heading towards the Glasgow Royal Infirmary. I don't really know why I was doing this, apart from the fact that I was looking for a job. I did not know where to go to get one and had no adult contact from whom I could seek appropriate advice.

As I was walking along, I saw several men going into a building obviously going back to work after lunch. I went into the building after them and saw a gentleman standing behind a desk. I asked him if he knew of any possibility of a summer job for a medical student. He said he did not know of any available jobs, as this was only the entrance to the factory building where the workers signed in.

As I was about to go out the door, he said to me, "Oh, son, why don't you try at the office? It's about thirty yards down the road."

I thanked him and made my way to the office building down the road as he'd advised.

On arriving there, I opened the door and found myself in a small building where two young ladies were filling in forms. One of them looked up at me and enquired, "Do you know what marital status means? I have to fill in this form but don't know the answer to this question?"

As I knew what the question meant, I was invited to sit down with them and started to look at and then fill out a form for what appeared to be for employment purposes. As I was doing this, a lady who was obviously a manageress judging from her dress, came into the room to collect the forms. Before I could apologise for being there, she said, "I thought there were meant to be two people here, not three. But never mind! Just leave the completed forms here."

I did so and then made my way home.

About a week or so later, I received a letter from the manageress congratulating me on being successful in obtaining a paid post for the summer with Collins, the publishers! She asked me to come and see her in her office before starting work. I could not believe it. I had a job! Praise God.

When I met up with her, she told me exactly what had happened. She told me that this post was one of the best a student could get in Glasgow. It was very well paid, and the working conditions were excellent. Something had happened in the past, and the grandfather Collins kept the factory going by using help from students. He, at that time, made a promise that there would always be several excellent posts for students to have over the summer holiday period. That promise had been kept for years.

Furthermore, she told me that she had received about 400 application forms and had to decide whom to employ. There were only about twenty posts for students in total. It was an extremely difficult task for her and caused her much stress.

She further informed me that, on the day she had to choose whom to employ, she was sitting at her desk wondering how to choose twenty students from such a large group of applicants. Just then the firm's chaplain, a local Church of Scotland minister, came in to see her. As he sat down in a chair in front of her, a wind came in through an open window and blew one form onto the floor. The minister picked it up and stated, "O, this belongs to Riaz Mohammed. I know him. I was playing football with him a week ago!"

"Well," she said, "given that recommendation from the chaplain, I could hardly turn you down!"

So, I was given a very well-paid summer job, which I hadn't even known existed. Not only that, the post was then offered to me for the rest of my six-year course at Glasgow University. It was an amazing answer to prayer.

As an official employee, not only was I well paid; I could also attend the staff cheap "book-buying day" every week. This allowed me to buy many books and Bibles very cheaply, some of which I gave to local charities, as well as sending some to places such as Russia.

Following advice from some ladies who worked there, I spoke to the manager of the factory. He oversaw all the work done by employees, and I asked him for, and was granted, two weeks' unpaid leave every year. This allowed me to have a holiday from work, which I used to assist at a Church of Scotland Seaside Mission. This not only gave me a holiday from work but also allowed me to tell people about Jesus. This experience reminded me that the Good Lord was in control of my life. I could put all my trust in Him!

My medical year class at Glasgow University consisted of about 220 medical students from all over the world. We were divided into two subgroups. These were called the "Western Infirmary" group and the "Glasgow Royal Infirmary" group. I, of course, joined the Royal Infirmary group. After all, I could walk to the Royal Infirmary from home and did not need a bus!

During my clinical studies, before going through the process of written examinations in medicine, I believed that I received a promise from God. This I shared with my fellow Christian medical student friends who were also in the Glasgow Royal Infirmary subgroup.

My Christian Medical student friends did not think much of the promise I had received. They did not think receiving such a promise was realistic. They certainly could not accept that such a promise was from God. We just had to agree to disagree!

The promise I received from God was this: The Lord said, if I were to be faithful and work hard at my studies, to the best of my abilities, I would pass all my examinations at the first sitting. I would not need to resit examinations and would not be required to study over the summer holiday period. This would allow me to earn income from my summer holiday job.

Everything seemed to go well. I managed to pass all examinations in the first, second, and third year of the course and had no resits! This was great, and I also had a continuing summer job to earn needed finance.

However, when it came to the fourth-year examination, which was crucial, as it was the final medical and surgical written examination of the course, something went very badly wrong! I was in a poor state of mind because of the number of pressures I was facing. The result was that my concentration was badly affected. I did very poorly on the examination. It was a multiple-choice paper, which gave one mark for a right answer and a minus one mark for a wrong answer. I was certain that I had failed that paper.

I went home after the examination for an Easter holiday break. It was a very difficult time for me. The evil one spoke to me saying, "God has let you down! He has not kept His promise when it really mattered. You have failed the final written medical examination! What could be worse?"

I had no answer to this suggestion.

I looked in my medical textbooks for the correct answers to any of the questions I could remember. And, often, I had given the wrong answer. There was no way round the problem that I could see. I had failed. Yet God had promised me that this would not happen!

The evil one suggested, continually, that God could not be trusted, even if He did exist! I was mad to put my trust in Him.

Well, I thought, *perhaps my Christian medical students were right after all.* But I could not set aside the thought that God would find a way!

After the Easter holidays, I went to the Glasgow Royal Infirmary, together with a hundred other students, to get our results. In those days, the results were posted on a public board for everyone to see. I was expecting to see my name with the word "failed" next to it.

To everyone's surprise, there were no results available on the first day back from the Easter holidays. There were no results posted on the second day; nor were there any on the third. Meanwhile, the other half of the year had had their examination results given as expected and had moved on to the next part of the course.

There was clearly some problem. Several representative students went to see the professor in charge, to ask what the problem was. He indicated that he would address the issue to the class the next day.

All the students were gathered in the Royal Infirmary lecture theatre awaiting some news. He came along and stated, "For the first time in the history of Glasgow University, which has been in existence for over five hundred years, a serious mistake has somehow been made! All the papers from the Royal Infirmary group have been incinerated by mistake before a single paper had been marked. So, the University Board has decided that you will all have to sit another examination."

Well, you can imagine how I felt. Whilst many other students were booing and throwing paper aeroplanes, I was praising God and saying,

"Get thee behind me Satan." These were the words that came to mind! God was the God of the second chance! He had given me another chance. I had not failed! If an examination paper has not been marked, one cannot legally fail that paper! Praise God.

As expected, our class met to sit another examination a week later. The same professor was there in charge and instructed the students to start the paper. Gradually, everyone noticed something was not as it should be and started to make all kinds of noises.

The professor stood up and said, "Those who are astute among you will have realised that the paper you have now to sit is the same paper you sat before! The university board has decided that there was not enough time to set a new paper for you, so you'd all sit the same paper again. So, there it is!"

I had, of course, spent several days during the Easter Holidays looking up the correct answers to the questions I could recall! I was, of course, thrilled when I was informed that I had passed that paper. In addition, I had no resits for the remainder of the six-year course, just as the Lord had promised! Praise God.

In my final year as a medical student, just before qualifying and becoming a doctor, I came across a patient I remember very well. I was part of a large team following consultant physicians in a ward round making important decisions about the continuing care of admitted patients. As the ward round was coming to an end, we came to a patient who was obviously dying. The sister on the ward round briefly told the consultants of the situation. To my astonishment, the whole team walked past the room without even opening the door! As I was passing the room at the very back of the group, I found that something inside me would not allow me to go past the room. I had to open the door, go inside, and say something to the dying patient.

As I approached the patient and asked her how she was feeling, she looked up and said, "I'm scared, doctor."

I was only a final year medical student but had a white coat on, which was why the patient called me "doctor". I sat down beside her, informed her who I was, and asked her what the problem was. She told me that she had a daughter who was causing her much concern. She was so upset that, despite the morphine injection, she just could not be comforted. She told me that her daughter had Down's syndrome, and she was concerned about her future welfare. How would she manage without her mum? This was the main reason for the patient's distress. She was not concerned about herself at all.

I told her honestly that there didn't appear to be anything more any of the doctors could do for her. That was probably why they had not come to see her. But I told her I knew of someone who could help. She asked me who that person was. I told her of the Great Physician, Jesus Christ, who could not only give her peace but could also look after her daughter, in ways that I could not even know about. He was worth trusting.

She looked at me and asked if I would pray for her and her daughter. I did so, and after this she accepted the Lord as her comforter and saviour. There then appeared on her face an immediate peace, which morphine could not give her. She fell asleep. This was on a Friday.

When I came back to the hospital the following Monday, she had peacefully passed away.

This incident reminded me that I was becoming a doctor to serve the Lord by helping people, not to make a great name for myself and be rich and important. I also learnt that there were many things in medicine, as in life, that only God could do. I should never underestimate the power of prayer.

CHAPTER 8

Experiences as a Doctor

I started my medical practise as a qualified doctor in the post of junior house officer on the 1 August 1974. In those days, it was compulsory to do one year as a junior house officer, spending six months in a surgical unit and six months in a medical unit. I hoped that, in time, I would specialise in surgery, with the thought that I would become a consultant surgeon in due course. There did not appear to be any reason why I could not do so. After all, I had come through the same teaching and training route as all others. And, whilst I was not in any way at the top of the class, I did seem to be competent and reasonably gifted as a doctor.

Having decided to specialise in surgery as my speciality, I thought it best to start as a junior house officer in general medicine, based in a district general hospital, before doing the surgical six months. It seemed to me best to acquire some more practical experience in clinical medicine, making any mistakes and learning from them, before taking on the post of junior house officer in surgery.

Also, I had planned to get married just after qualification and needed a place to stay. A junior house officer post in a district general hospital provided that more easily than did a post in a more competitive teaching hospital.

Things worked out well. I obtained married accommodation in the hospital where I was offered a junior hospital medical post. This made things so much easier.

Thereafter, I was also successful in gaining a six-month post in surgery in a teaching hospital in Glasgow. This seemed a better option, as progression to higher surgical training was extremely competitive, and having support from senior consultants from a teaching hospital was more likely to lead to success in obtaining suitable training posts in surgery in the future. I was also blessed in obtaining married accommodation in that teaching hospital too. This gave my wife and me the opportunity to save some money over a year to allow us to purchase a small car and obtain a mortgage to buy a house of our own to live in. God is faithful.

After completing my six-month junior hospital post in surgery, I was supported by the chief consultant surgeon in pursuing a career in surgery. He knew me, as I had previously been a student in his unit and must have impressed him well enough to receive his support.

His advice was that I should compete for a post as a temporary lecturer in anatomy at Glasgow University, as this subject was recognised as the most difficult to pass in the forthcoming surgical examinations. Whilst this did mean leaving full-time clinical medicine for a year, he took the view that this was the best way to proceed in surgery. I took his advice, and with his support as my referee, I was successful in obtaining a post as a lecturer in anatomy at the University of Glasgow for one year.

To become a surgeon, it was necessary to pass the appropriate examinations of one of the surgical colleges in the United Kingdom. The first part of the surgical examinations was called the primary FRCS (Fellowship of the Royal College of Surgeons). This was a very difficult examination to pass, and of the three examination subjects, consisting of anatomy, pathology and physiology, most experts in the field took the view that anatomy was perhaps the most difficult. A full-time post as an anatomy demonstrator would allow me to learn more about human anatomy, as well as gain experience in teaching medical students. This would be the best way to prepare for the examinations to come. Once this examination was out of the way, I could then progress onto further recognised training in surgery.

Things progressed well, and I had a very interesting year going back to the university as an anatomy demonstrator. I got to know well one of the other demonstrators, who had qualified with me and was also a Christian believer. I was fortunate enough to pass the primary FRCS examination on the first attempt. Then, after successfully competing for a three-year training post, I started training in surgery in teaching hospitals in the West of Scotland.

Following two years of further surgical training, I decided to sit the final FRCS examination of the surgical college known as the Royal College of Surgeons and Physicians of Glasgow. Whilst this was the earliest possible opportunity for me to be allowed to take the examination, having fulfilled all necessary requirements, I decided to do so. I felt that I was ready, and my consultant supervisors agreed that was the case. I was delighted when I passed that examination at the first attempt, thus becoming a fellow of the Royal College of Surgeons. From now on, I would be known as "Mr Mohammed", rather than "Dr Mohammed".

In addition to passing surgical examinations, it was, of course, necessary to learn from consultant supervisors how to perform surgical procedures and to look after patients with surgical problems.

I remember as a senior house officer, some two years or so after qualifying, performing my first appendectomy operation on my own. I, as required, informed my supervising consultant of the need of this emergency operation on a five-year-old girl. I thought she could not wait till the next day. The consultant told me over the telephone to go ahead and perform the procedure. He would be available should I needed any assistance.

This was a seminal moment for me. All my colleagues knew I was going to theatre on my own for the first time and all wished me good luck! I am glad to say that the diagnosis was correct, and the operation went well. Afterwards, that little girl had the very best of post-operative care to ensure there were no further problems! It was an utter delight to see her recover well and go home back to her family.

In addition to learning the basics of safe surgery, I discovered the importance of praying for my patients. I recall operating on a patient with gastric obstruction when I was still a trainee senior house officer. I performed a bypass procedure to allow the obstructed stomach to empty into the small bowel, thus relieving her of her vomiting. I could have asked for assistance from the on-call consultant, who would have been available to come to theatre, but decided that I could do the operation on my own. It was very much a matter of judgement as to when a trainee could complete a surgical procedure without assistance from someone more senior.

The operation seemed to go well, and I was able to explain to the consultant and the patient the next day what had been done. We then all waited for the patient to improve. She did not! Her stomach just would not empty. The consultants said that, in their experience, they had seen this before and that these things occasionally happened. Sometimes, for unknown reasons, many days passed before the stomach started to empty.

As the days went on, she became more unwell. I began to wonder whether I had done the operation correctly and to think that, perhaps, I should have sought the consultant's advice after all. But then again, one must make these important decisions at some point during the training period! However, it also remains the case that trainees will not get it right on every occasion. I therefore wondered if, on this occasion, I had done something wrong.

As time went on, the possibility of reoperation became more and more real. I felt sorry for myself, as I felt as though I was under scrutiny. However, I felt even sorrier for my patient. I did not want her to go through another difficult and possibly life-threatening procedure. What could I do? It was then that I started to pray for my patient. I should have, of course, done so earlier!

When I did start praying for the lady, something seemed to change. The very next day, when I went back into the ward, she was sitting up and eating. Her symptoms had all gone. Of course, all the consultants said this happens occasionally. Things sometimes go more slowly than expected. That may well be true, but for me, praying for my patients became a habit, which I did not ever regret!

This training period was a very busy and difficult time for all the surgical trainees, with a long hard week being the norm. For example, for one year working in a busy district general hospital as a surgical registrar, I would leave the house for the hospital on a Friday morning and not return home till Monday evening. This happened for a whole year every third weekend, as there were three of us registrars sharing on-call duty. In addition, we were also covering night duty, one night in three during the rest of the week. All this was in addition to the 9 a.m. to 5 p.m. normal working day from Monday to Friday. This meant that we all worked an average of about ninety hours per week.

It was during this difficult training period as a surgical registrar that I began to wonder what the future held for me in surgery. Was I good enough to make it to a consultant position? I suppose a type of professional depression came over me. I don't know why, but I began to wonder if God loved me. And, if He did not, I could not really blame Him for not doing so. I was not even a good person, never mind a good Christian doctor.

As I was going through these feelings, which I did not share with anyone, I had to operate on a little boy who was about three years of age. He had a major lifelong problem. He had been born with a congenital problem resulting in too much fluid in the brain. Because of this, he was mentally disabled and had very poor quality of life. He was in and out of hospital quite frequently.

The nursing staff knew him well, as they had nursed him many times in the past. I heard them say that they were sorry to see him being readmitted yet again. They also seemed to suggest that it would be best if he were to die, as he had no quality of life and had no chance of any improvement. I agreed with them that their judgement was clinically correct.

He'd had a valve inserted into the brain some months earlier to allow brain fluid to drain into a vein. This drain had blocked, and it was my duty to take him to theatre and replace the valve.

This I did on the night he was admitted and then awaited events. His condition did not improve, and sadly, the next day, he died. The nurses were sad for the family but glad to see this "worthless life" finally come to an end. I kind of agreed with that point of view. I must confess that, feeling myself to be nothing more than a stranger and a foreigner, in some way, I saw myself as being not dissimilar to this boy, whose life was not worth living.

It was my duty to tell the parents that their son had passed away. As I did so, the mother just burst into tears and could not be comforted. The father, upset as he obviously was, asked me if it were possible for him to see the body. I said that this would not be a problem. As he left the room to see the body, he stopped at the door and turned around to me and asked if I would be prepared to accompany him. I was happy to do so.

As we approached the boy's room, we could see through the glass window a small cot in the middle of the room with the body covered by a white sheet.

As we approached the body, the father asked if he could remove the white sheet. I said that would not be a problem. He did so and then asked me if he could pick up the body. Once again, I said that would not be a problem.

He then picked up the body and, with tears in his eyes, began to cry and said, "Michael, my son. How am I going to live without you? I love you so much. Oh, Michael, my son, my son."

I had to leave that room, to prevent bursting into tears myself.

However, this father taught me something that I needed to learn about love. To everyone else, Michael was just a "useless body", with no quality of life and no future. Whilst that was perhaps true, nevertheless, to the father, Michael was still a precious son and was loved with a true father's love.

Through this incident, I discovered that God was saying to me that it did not matter what others thought of me. Even if others saw me as a useless person, and even if they were right in their judgement, God still loved with an eternal love. I should never ever doubt that!

I also concluded that working with young children in paediatric surgery was not the speciality for me. This was mainly because I could not dissociate myself enough from the emotional involvement, which was required to be objective in the clinical care of young children.

After completing my three years of surgical registrar training, I was advised that I now needed to do some full-time surgical research in order to improve my C.V. Thereafter, I would then, hopefully, qualify for a post known as senior surgical registrar. This very competitive post was the one I needed to acquire prior to becoming a consultant in general surgery.

Suitable research posts were very few and, naturally, very competitive. I was fortunate enough to be given an opportunity to discuss matters with a professor of surgery at the Glasgow Royal Infirmary. He agreed that doing full-time research in surgery was the best way forward for me and was kind enough to offer me an excellent research post. Unfortunately, this would involve me going to America for a year to carry out research there.

Whilst this was an excellent opportunity, I was not able to accept the offer. The reason was that my wife was expecting our second child and was close to the time of delivery. If I were to accept this research post based in the United States, I would have to go there, and that would mean leaving her on her own for several months. I was not prepared to accept that.

There was at that time one other research post, based in Glasgow, which seemed ideal for me. It so happened that there were two other registrars also after this post. All three of us were Christians and knew one another well. I found out, after the interview, that I was second in line and would only be offered the post if the person who was considered first did not accept it. I knew the person very well, having worked with him at the same hospital. He was a bit older and had more surgical experience than me. Interestingly, he was also being interviewed for a senior registrar post in paediatric surgery about the same time. I would only be successful in obtaining the research post I needed if he were to be successful in obtaining the paediatric post instead.

I began to pray over this issue. I wanted the best for us all but had no power to make it happen. But I believed that, in God's providence, things would work out. After waiting for about a week, I got the news that the research post was mine. The other candidate had been successful in obtaining the paediatric senior registrar post and was happy to accept it, rather than the research post. This meant that I could stay in Glasgow and be there for my wife and our children.

I started the research post in August 1980, based in the surgical academic unit in the Western Infirmary, Glasgow, headed by Professor Sir Andrew Watt Kay. He was a well-known world authority in surgical research related to gastric and duodenal ulceration. What an opportunity!

After some initial problems getting started in surgical research, I finally got an opportunity to study the effects of a new drug, which was thought to reduce stomach acid and was useful in healing duodenal and gastric ulcers. My research studies went extremely well, so much so that I was successful in publishing some of my research data in recognised medical journals.

It was also wonderful for me to look at human tissue through the electron microscope as part of my research studies. This instrument can magnify up to 100 times greater than the better-known light microscope, which can itself magnify up to 2,000 times normal. Without the electron microscope, no human eye could ever see the detail that is present in the cells of the lining of the human stomach, which produce gastric acid.

The beauty that was there to be observed was just stunning. The form and function of the cells producing acid was so logically designed that I could not help but feel that God had left his thumbprint there for humankind to discover, centuries before humankind even thought of the electron microscope. How great an artistic creator God we have!

Whilst using the electron microscope to study individual cells closely, I discovered some changes in the cells of patients taking the drug, which could have been interpreted as precancerous. As some authors, had published medical articles suggesting that these types of acid-reducing drugs could give rise to gastric cancer, I considered submitting some of my data for publication. This would undoubtedly have been very controversial. It could have meant that a drug firm that had been selling a very similar drug for healing ulcers may have had to remove it from the market, causing much concern to patients who had taken these drugs for some years. This was a very interesting dilemma. Should I just "publish or perish" as they say in the research world? What to do?

As I was thinking about this problem, I was approached by a nationally known professor of medicine who also worked in the same hospital. He had heard me speak on this issue at one of our research meetings. He suggested that it might be wise not to publish such controversial data. It was likely to cause much distress to millions of people who had taken the drug and would potentially cost millions of pounds to the company involved. This professor of medicine was, at that time, chairman of the NHS Committee on Safety of Medicines (CSM) which had been set up to advise the British government on new medicines. I listened to his advice and decided not to submit the data for publication.

Sometime later, I was approached by a drug representative for the other drug firm, who told me that his firm was keen to have access to my data that had not been submitted for publication. How he knew about my data remains a mystery. An offer was made for cash to be put into a Swiss bank account if the data could be released to him. On hearing of this offer, I ended the conversation immediately, as this was clearly not an ethical thing to do. It did show to me, however, a part of research that is ruthless and not often mentioned! I am pleased to say that, as the years went on, accumulated data showed no evidence that the acid-reducing drugs were cancerous.

As was customary in the research unit, I presented some of the results of my studies to a staff meeting attended by several professors, which included Professor Kay. I received a very positive accolade for the data I was producing and was encouraged to go on with my research. I was also keen to show the data at an international medical meeting in Sweden. However, my research supervisor was not keen for me to do so. He suggested that it would be much better for me to keep the data and update it before presenting it at a much more important research meeting in the United States of America. He would make the arrangements for this to happen. I felt that I had no choice but to follow that advice. I, therefore, did not submit my results for presentation in Sweden.

It was some months later I discovered by chance that some of my data had, in fact, been presented in Sweden. My supervisor and two of his colleagues had attended the meeting without my knowledge. Such is the way of medical research at times. It did make me feel a little more like a foreigner and stranger in this life. And, of course, the trip to the United States never materialised.

The one major problem I had to face was that my appointment to the research post was for one year only. This was not enough time for me to turn my surgical research papers and academic presentations into a possible thesis, giving me the opportunity to submit for a Doctorate of Medicine (MD) to Glasgow University. This post-graduate degree is one of the highest degrees that a university can grant in Medicine. My research studies had gone so well that I was sure that writing an MD thesis was possible, though, of course, I needed to spend much more time working at it.

As I was thinking and praying about what to do, I naturally spoke to several of my senior colleagues to see what ideas they might have. It soon became clear that the amount of time needed to complete the research would not allow me to take on a standard clinical post in the place of the current full-time research post. I needed an extension to my contract as the best way forward.

On seeking advice from my senior mentor, I found that he took a different view. He suggested that it would be best for me not to consider going down this route at all, as it was not necessary. Others thought that his view was wholly wrong; they thought that the advice given by my senior mentor was because he had never gained such a postgraduate degree himself, despite being in full-time research for many years. It was difficult to know what was best. I just had to pray about the matter and leave it in God's hands.

As it so happened, on a Saturday morning following the research study presentation I had given, I met Professor Kay at the hospital going to do a ward round. This required using an old-fashioned lift to reach the floor where the patients were housed. The lift required the door to be physically opened. I opened the door for the professor, and both of us got onto the lift. Then quite unexpectedly, the professor asked me what I was thinking of doing with my ongoing research studies. And was I considering writing an MD thesis?! Having seen some of the data I had presented at the meeting, he thought I had made a very good start towards that possibility. There had been no MD thesis submitted by the permanent research staff of the unit for many years. This was not good for the reputation of his research department.

I indicated that, much as I would love to do so, I did not have enough time to even consider writing an MD thesis. I only had a one-year contract, and this was about to come to an end.

The professor simply looked at me and said: "No problem. I will arrange for you to stay on a year longer."

So, that is what happened. The professor ensured I was given another year's contract, which allowed me to finish my research studies and then subsequently write and submit my thesis for a successful outcome! Thanks, Professor!

When I finished my two years in full-time research, I was ready to compete for a post as senior surgical registrar. This was not easy to get, as the competition was naturally very severe. In addition, it was essential to gain a suitable senior registrar post within the limited time that we all had as surgical registrars. Otherwise our potential careers as consultant surgeons would come to an early end. That's how things were then! A close Christian friend of mine was at a similar stage in his career as me and was also competing for a senior registrar post. We were, in fact, often competing for the same posts in the Glasgow area.

I only had my wife to share my concerns with but did not wish to burden her with all the possibilities that existed and found this time very hard. I had always felt that it was God's will that I should become a consultant general surgeon, but was I wrong? Was I just imagining things? What would I do if my career failed to progress further? What other options were available for me? There did not appear to be an easy answer to these questions.

Then one evening, I was invited to give my testimony at a meeting of the Gideons' Society. At this meeting, I met a gentleman who had a prominent role with the Gideons. It turned out that this godly gentleman was the father of my dear friend who was also competing for the same posts as me. What my friend's father said that night was a true word from God! He told me that he was sure that the Lord would not have brought both his son and me thus far in our surgical career only to let us down. He was sure that God had a plan for both of us. He then went on to say that he was, naturally, praying for his son. And then, to my astonishment, he went on to reassure me that he was praying for me too! I was a foreigner and a stranger in this world, but God made sure that I knew I was not entirely alone. I did have friends who cared and prayed for me from within His church family!

As it turned out, I was successful in obtaining a senior registrar post very soon after this meeting. Among those serving on the appointment committee for this post, in the providence of God, was the consultant surgeon who I'd worked for when I first did my surgical house officer post—the one who had advised me to do anatomy at Glasgow University. My mentor from Professor Kay's unit was also serving on the committee. He was the one who'd kindly phoned me after the interview to advise me that I had been successful in obtaining the senior registrar post. What wonderful news! I was now on my way to a career as consultant in general surgery. Praise God!

My friend had also applied for the post in Glasgow but did not get on the short list for interview. This was deeply disappointing for him. Yet he was kind enough to congratulate me on my success. However, some months later, my Christian friend was also successful in obtaining a senior registrar post, although, in the Lord's will, this turned out to be in England. God had answered his father's prayers for us both.

CHAPTER 9

A Sad 'Accident'

Having obtained a senior registrar post, I greatly enjoyed learning and practising surgery on a higher level. For me, clearly, this was the way forward and within the will of God. Happy days!

I remember an occasion when I was working for a consultant surgeon who was extremely busy. Because of his workload, he had a very large waiting list of patients, which he just did not have time to deal with. The waiting list was getting larger every week and had been a problem for some years. I came up with an idea to deal with this problem. The solution was simple. With his knowledge and consent, I would operate on his patients on a Friday afternoon operating session that no one else was keen to use. He was happy for me to go ahead and do this. Not only would that be good for his patients, it would also give me more operating experience. This worked far better than anyone expected, and within a year or so, he told me that he was delighted to have no waiting list for the first time in years.

Some of my friends thought I was not being wise, in that I could have had at least some Friday afternoons off if I did not have recognised duties to do. Hence, some of my weekends off could start on a Friday afternoon. Whilst there was some merit in that point of view, little did I know at the time that this experience would be very valuable in years to come when I would be appointed to a post of clinical director for surgical services and would have the responsibility of reducing long surgical waiting lists.

After about four years of further senior registrar training in specialities such as general surgery, urology, and vascular surgery in various hospitals under the supervision of several different consultants in the West of Scotland, I naturally began to think about obtaining a suitable consultant post. After all, I had fulfilled all legal requirements to do so. I was now fully qualified and ready to move on. General surgery seemed the best option for me, even though it was perhaps the most competitive of the various specialities I had trained in.

I prayed to the Lord to place me wherever He wished but also asked that I would be part of a team of at least three consultant surgeons rather than a smaller unit with fewer consultants. In addition, my other wish was that, if possible, I would have one other consultant surgeon colleague who was a Christian to work with. That would be great.

With these thoughts in mind, I was visiting my friend who had very recently obtained a consultant surgeon's post in Yorkshire. I was, of course, delighted for him, even though his future career would now be in England. I was expecting that I would soon be obtaining a consultant post myself, which was likely to be somewhere in the West of Scotland. This would be my first choice. Exciting times indeed!

On coming home from visiting my friend, I decided to give my wife's car a quick run. This was to make sure that her car battery was fully charged, as it lost its charge quite frequently. It was an old Ford Fiesta Firefly. This was on a Saturday morning when I had little else to do, and Janet was busy making breakfast for the family anyway. A quick drive down a country road before breakfast seemed a good use of time. I did not bother to push the car seat back to give my longer legs more room. I was only intending to go for a short country run and would be back in ten minutes for breakfast anyway!

As I was driving along a quiet narrow country road not far from our house, I saw a police car overtaking other vehicles and coming straight towards me at an extremely high speed. The emergency blue light was on and flashing. It seemed obvious that the policeman in the driver's seat was going to an emergency. I looked to my right and saw a van, which the police car was clearly thinking of overtaking. I looked to the left and only saw a wall, so there was no prospect of turning to the left. Just as I feared, the police car came straight for me. The driver could not have seen my car due to the bend of the road and the speed at which he was driving. This resulted in a head-to-head crash.

I felt the front of the car coming towards me. As I had not pulled the car seat back, my leg was in the way, and this stopped my chest from being crushed. The price I paid for my life was a badly damaged right leg. As the police car crashed into my car, time just seemed to stand still. I could not see or hear anything. It was like looking through a small window into eternity. The only other thing I remember doing was saying, "Help me, Lord. Help me."

I was informed later that my head had hit the windscreen, and fortunately, the windscreen had just flown out in one piece. Whilst this caused a large wound on my forehead, it would have been far worse had the glass screen shattered. As I recovered from the initial shock, I found I was trapped in the car and could not get out. However, when a policeman came over to see me, the first thing I apparently asked was concerning anyone else who may have been hurt so that I could help!

I had to be cut out of the car by the fire brigade and taken to the nearest hospital for further treatment. Whilst I was waiting to be taken out of the car, a male nurse happened to be passing that way. He came over to see me, and though there was nothing he could do, he knew what had happened. This proved to be quite helpful later when Janet phoned the hospital to find out what had happened to me. He was able to speak to her and give her some useful information.

I was taken by ambulance to the A & E department of the nearest hospital, where I was examined by a consultant anaesthetist who happened to know me. She made sure that the consultant orthopaedic surgeon on duty was not allowed to go home, as he had to treat my injuries immediately! Also, I could go directly to the anaesthetic room for any necessary surgical treatment, as I had not had any breakfast that morning, and so my stomach was empty.

It turned out that my right femur had been crushed and broken in three places. But this had saved my life, as it had prevented my chest from being crushed. I was told afterwards that the fractures were so unusual that the most appropriate metal stent that was required to treat me was no longer routinely made. However, if the appropriate manufacturers were given six months' notice, they would make one specifically on demand.

The consultant thought this type of stent was the best option to treat my fractures. The registrar who was on duty with the consultant for that weekend told me later that he did not normally work with the duty consultant. He was registrar to another consultant who was not on duty that weekend. However, that surgeon had decided that it would be useful to order such a stent some six month earlier, just in case it was needed. So, there was a stent somewhere in the theatre stores. Even the theatre sister was not aware of this. The registrar was asked to un-scrub and to have a look around, in the hope of finding the necessary stent.

He did so and managed to find it. He brought it to the operating consultant. Miraculously, it fitted perfectly—almost as if it had been made for my needs. This way of dealing with my fractures allowed for a much swifter healing and quicker return to mobility than other means would have.

The next day, on awakening from the anaesthetic and sleep, I looked at my right ankle and knew right away that it was badly broken. Somehow this had been missed. I brought this to the attention of the ward sister and was swiftly taken back to theatre. I needed another anaesthetic to have my ankle fixed with screws. My consultant later apologised to me for missing my ankle injury. I said that there was no need for an apology. I was just grateful to him for the treatment he had given me and for helping to save my life. Nothing was more important than that! We all make mistakes. Only God makes none.

Despite serious injury, I had survived the accident. One orthopaedic consultant told me later that, given the velocity involved (which would have been at least 90 miles per hour for the police car and 30 miles per hour from me, meaning a combined velocity of 120 miles per hour), in his considerable experience, I should not have survived! My thigh bone saved my life by getting in the way, as I had not shifted the car seat back! Interestingly, being intentionally lazy can be a good thing sometimes.

The post-operative period for me was, not unexpectedly, very difficult and painful—not only physically but also emotionally and spiritually. I thought that, as I was a deacon in my local church at the time, it was necessary to ask our church secretary to inform the congregation I had not done anything wrong to cause the accident. I had not been speeding. I had not been in the wrong place on the road. And I had not been under the influence of alcohol or any such thing. I wanted the congregation to know this, as I did not want any disgrace to come upon the church because of some suspected wrong action by one of its deacons.

After a day or two had passed following the operation, I asked for my frequent morphine injections to be stopped. Because of the side effects of the morphine, I just did not feel real, and I wanted to face reality. This was done promptly as requested. Instead of Morphine, I was given paracetamol!

One night, whilst in considerable pain and distress, I looked up at the ceiling. Only a small table lamp was left on. In the lamplight, I could see the shadow of my bed reflected onto the ceiling. In addition, the various poles and gadgets of my orthopaedic bed also threw shadows onto the ceiling. The shadows reminded me clearly of our Lord on the Cross. In my pain and distress at the time, I could imagine just a little of what the Lord would have experienced when he hung on the cross for you and for me.

As I began to recover from the immediate life-threatening situation I had been in, I suppose, quite naturally, I began to wonder why all this had happened to me. I began to ask, Had God abandoned me to this incident because He did not love me anymore? To make matters worse, I could not think of a reason why He should have loved me anyway! I was the worst of sinners in the sight of a Holy God. Whilst this thought troubled me greatly, I did not share it with anyone. I became me more and more depressed. I, once again, felt that I was a foreigner and stranger in this life and was all alone.

Given the severity of my clinical condition, my two children were not allowed to see me for several days. In the meanwhile, my daughter Sylvia, who would have been about six years old at the time, decided to write her daddy a letter. She, I found out later, did not discuss this with anyone, including her mother. She just did it independently. After writing the note, she put her letter in an envelope and asked her mum to give it to me. No one, including her mum, knew what Sylvia had written till I told her later.

As the news of my accident became known, due to the kindness of church friends and acquaintances, I received daily many, many letters— in fact, so many that it was not possible for me to read them all till much after the event. I did, however, read my daughter's letter. I had to read that!

When I did read what she had written, my heart broke! For in that letter, written by my six-year-old daughter, with no help from anyone human, I read, "God loves you! God loves me. Do you love the Son? Well I do!"

I could hardly read these words due to the tears in my eyes. Here was the Lord's answer to the question I had raised only in my mind, about God's love for a sinner like me. No one else could have reached my heart more deeply than my little daughter. God used her graciously to speak to me in a situation, which I felt no one else could have done. The answer was clear. No matter what had happened or why it had happened, God still loved me!

As I began to recover from my injuries, before I was allowed by my consultant to get out of bed, I began to wonder about the possible level of my recovery. I was deeply concerned on reflection that, when I became a consultant surgeon, I would have to stand for hours to do major surgical operations. Would I be able to do so adequately for the safety of my patients and for my own comfort? This became another worrying issue for me. I suppose being a patient when you are also a doctor is not always easy!

The consultant orthopaedic surgeon who was looking after me told me that he was about to take a weekend off. But before going away, he wanted to share something with me. He knew from the number of cards I had received from various churches that I had a Christian faith and that I believed in the Bible as the Word of God. He suggested that I should read the Bible verses that mentioned something about "on eagle's wings".

I recognised the verses that he was referring to and looked them up. It was taken from the book of Isaiah, which states: -

Hast thou not known? hast thou not heard, that the everlasting God, the Lord, the Creator of the ends of the earth, fainteth not, neither is weary? there is no searching of his understanding.

He giveth power to the faint; and to them that have no might he increaseth strength.

Even the youths shall faint and be weary, and the young men shall utterly fall:

But they that wait upon the Lord shall renew their

strength; they shall mount up with wings as eagles; they shall run, and not be weary; and they shall walk, and not faint. (Isaiah 40:28–31, KJV)

I was delighted to read this and was overcome with relief because the Lord was saying to me that, not only would I be given "strength" to "stand" long enough for operations, I would also be able to "walk" and even "run".

I shared this great news with anyone who was interested. All the nursing staff agreed that this message was indeed very relevant and encouraging.

When my wife came to see me that day, I told her about this scripture and how great it was. I found that, despite everything I said, she was really "not taking it in". She only listened to me out of courtesy and was more concerned about how I was recovering now, not too bothered about any difficulty that may be ahead. Although she acknowledged the biblical words I was telling her about, she did not seem to take them on board and rejoice with me as I had hoped she would have done.

I found out later what happened after she went home. She was very busy looking after our two children by herself and answering the phone to talk to people who kept phoning to kindly enquire after me. At the end of the night, she decided to put the phone off the hook, have a bath, and just relax.

After the bath, when she was finally feeling relaxed, she decided to do something she had never done before. She simply switched on the radio, late at night. She didn't know why she did this and had no thought as to what she would be listening to. She had no idea which channel would come on. She had never done this before.

As soon as she switched on the radio, out came a booming, loud, male voice saying, "But those who wait for the Lord shall renew their strength, they shall mount up with wings like eagles, they shall run and not be weary, they shall walk and not faint."

She immediately fell on her knees before God. In tears, she thanked God, realising that God had, in fact, graciously spoken to her to convey a message about her husband's future when she was finally ready to listen! He did this through the radio!

Things went well post-operation, and I was privileged to be visited by the consultant urologist with whom I was working at the time. He was in America when the accident happened, but as soon as he arrived home, his wife told him what had happened to me. He immediately made his way to the hospital, even though he was suffering from jet lag and came to see how I was and whether there was anything he could do. Also, I had a visit from three consultant surgeons from the hospital I was assigned to as senior registrar. They came to see me and to reassure me that they would do whatever was required for my well-being.

These visits were very helpful and reminded me that, even though many would have considered me nothing but a foreigner and stranger in this world, I was not completely alone. There were some who genuinely cared for me. However, I was, by this time, having so many visitors from everywhere that the consultant decided it was too much for me and not in my best interest. As a temporary measure, he announced that I could only have relatives visit. Everyone had to obey that order. He was the consultant in charge after all!

It was interesting for me to be a patient rather than a doctor in a hospital setting. I found, for example, that the hospital food was, for me, tasteless and not very appetising. I had, of course, lost a great deal of weight. My wife thought it would be best to contact my elder brother to see if some homemade Pakistani food could be brought to the hospital for me. As they were relatives, my brother and his family could come and see me.

My brother and his wife were delighted to help. I soon discovered that the food they brought was much more to my taste and much more easily consumed. They were astonished to see the number of cards and flowers I had received from all over the country. Perhaps they had thought I would have very little support from anyone, as I was, by this time, no longer part of the Asian community, having become a Christian years ago. I got the impression that they were surprised and very impressed by the obvious concern and support given to me by Christian friends from all over the country.

Sometime later, as I was beginning to recover, my son and daughter were finally allowed to visit me. When I saw them for the first time after the accident, I noticed that my son looked very serious and seemed to ignore everything. I could see right away that he just wanted to speak to me. I, therefore, decided to ignore everyone else and spoke to him as if there was no one else present. I asked him if there was anything he wanted to know.

He simply looked straight at me and asked, in a very concerned voice, if I was going to die. Clearly this thought was dominating his young eight-year-old mind. I reassured him that I was not going to die.

The next question from his lips was that he had noticed my broken right leg looked stronger than my normal left leg. Why was that? I explained that my right broken leg was extremely swollen because fluid was taking longer to drain from it. It was thicker looking for that reason only but would get back to normal in time.

As soon as he had obtained answers to his questions, he just reverted to being a normal eight-year-old boy, who just wanted to run around seeing interesting things in the ward!

Meanwhile, I noticed that my six-year-old daughter had sat still on the floor and just kept looking up at me. I smiled and waved at her as though she was the only person in the room. She shyly smiled back and then went off happily with the nurses to see the things they wanted to show her. It was heart-warming to see my family, even though the circumstances were awful.

I seemed to make good progress, with the help of the physiotherapist, and was soon allowed to go home on two crutches, providing I could make my own arrangements for safe transport home. There was a problem, however. I was not able to bend my right leg and, therefore, needed transport that was big enough for my needs. We always had rather small cars, as I did not favour large vehicles. I took the view that, as Christians, we should be extremely careful with climate change and such things. I held the view that having a large car was never appropriate. Fortunately, one member of our church did have a large car and offered to drive me home. Had it not been for this gracious offer, I would have had to spend a lot longer in the hospital. I did not want to stay away from my family any longer than necessary, so I accepted the offer. I learnt that, sometimes, people choose to do things differently, and I need to be, perhaps, a little less judgemental of others.

Because of the injuries I had sustained, I was off work completely for six months. As I was on an NHS contract, this meant I would be paid my basic salary for six months—providing, of course, my GP was able to declare that I was not fit to go back to work sooner. This was not a problem.

However, the rules and regulations laid down that, after the six-month period was over, I would be granted only half of my basic salary for another six months before having no further salary at all. Given my financial circumstances, I had no choice but to go back to work after the first six-month period was over.

This meant I had to be driven to hospital by my wife, and I still needed two sticks to allow me to get around. I was delighted when my consultant colleagues and other staff accepted the situation and gave me work that I could manage despite my disability. As things progressed well, I was then able to manage with one stick for another six months, before not requiring any. It therefore took me about eighteen months to get back to normality.

It was very interesting to find out later from the nursing staff that the patients often referred to me as the "crippled doctor" and were very happy to speak to me about some things they would not mention to the other medical staff. I suppose they saw me as not only a doctor but also a fellow patient.

Several months after the accident, I received communication from a procurator fiscal in Glasgow. He indicated his intentions to take the policeman who was driving the police car to court because of the accident that had occurred, whilst he was driving with his emergency lights on. This meant I would be required to attend as a principle witness. I did say that, as a doctor, I understood that accidents could happen and asked, Can one really put all the blame on someone responding to an emergency? After all, you might, in the future, be the person needing police assistance. The procurator fiscal's reply was that it was up to the judge to decide the matter and no one else. So, together with others who'd been present when the accident had taken place, I had to attend as a witness.

Very sadly, at the trial, evidence came to light to show that the policeman was not responding to an emergency at all. He was simply showing off to his fellow police officer. He wanted to frighten his friend and demonstrate how great a driver he was.

In the policeman's defence, I was delighted to hear the QC representing him agreeing that I was not responsible, in any way, for what happened and that there was no way I could have avoided the accident. He agreed that I was on the correct side of the road and not driving illegally in any way. The problem was caused entirely by the policeman's driving, and his defence was that, in general, police should be allowed to drive as they thought best given the circumstances they faced.

After all the evidence was heard, we all waited for the judge to give his decision. To my surprise, the policeman was finally found guilty of "reckless" driving. This was a serious offence. His punishment consisted of eight penalty points on his driving licence and a fine of £250.

There were several police officers attending the hearing. As soon as the verdict was announced by the judge, to my surprise, all the police officers left the court so that the guilty police officer was left alone with his QC. The QC then approached me to shake my hand and wish me all the best for the future. He also apologised for what he had to do but said that it was his duty to represent the policeman. He then left the court as well.

Immediately after this, only the guilty policeman and I were left outside the courtroom. Everyone had departed through an automatic door. As I made my way towards the door, something happened. The Lord spoke to me in a way I could not ignore. He said, "You have been forgiven so much. Can you not forgive?"

At that point, I could not go out the door without speaking to the guilty policeman. I approached the policeman and shook his hand. With tears in my eyes, I said to him that I very much hoped that he would never, ever do such a foolish thing again! At this point, the police officer with real emotion, thanked me for speaking to him and told me that I did not know how much my doing that meant to him.

I did not see him again. But a few years later, when I was doing an outpatient clinic, I came across a patient who was a police officer. He recognised me and knew about the accident I'd had with the police car. He informed me that the policeman responsible for the accident was the subject of an internal police disciplinary hearing, following which he was dismissed from the police force!

Through my legal representation, I was financially compensated for the pain and suffering I had endured. Whilst this was reasonable, I insisted that the National Health Service should also be recompensed by the police insurance company for the six months' salary I was paid whilst on sick leave. I felt quite strongly that the NHS should not be responsible for paying me sick leave for six months, given that the policeman had been found guilty of reckless driving. Sometime later, I was glad to hear from my lawyer that the insurance company had finally agreed to do this.

I am pleased to say that, over time, I made a very good recovery—so much so that I took part in a five-kilometre community race in Newton Mearns some years later. Not only was I able to finish in a reasonably good time, I am also proud to say that I beat my very fit, healthy, and experienced race running twenty-five-year-old daughter!

Although my health did improve considerably as time went on, unfortunately, there remains a minor problem. I have the metal stent in my leg and will do so for the rest of my life! Every time I go through airport security, I set off the detectors and have to indicate that it is the metal plate in my right leg that causes the problem! On one occasion, at Heathrow Airport, I had to go into a private room and take my trousers off so that the scar on my leg could be examined. Small price to pay for your life and health!

CHAPTER 10

Obtaining My Consultant Surgeon's Post

aving lost about a year or so from ill health because of the car crash,
I got back to normal medical practise and had no difficulty carrying
out all my duties. It was now the right time to start applying for a
suitable consultant post. I hoped to gain a post, preferably in the West of
Scotland, where I had been fully trained to consultant level. My speciality
was general surgery, with a special interest in gastrointestinal surgery. It
certainly was a very competitive area of surgical practise, but I was quietly
confident that I would soon be successful in obtaining a suitable post. A
post in or around Glasgow would be ideal. We would not have to move
to a new house and could continue to worship at the same church that
we as a family had become accustomed to.

I found this time to be much more difficult and distressing then I
had ever expected. Despite several interviews for local consultant posts,
I was unsuccessful. I found it increasingly discouraging when I was
told repeatedly after the interviews that I was very unlucky in coming
"second", yet again!

After about two years of unsuccessful interviews, not including
numerous occasions when I did not even make the short list, I began
to wonder if something was badly wrong. I saw all my contemporaries
appointed ahead of me and then began to see surgeons who were junior to
me being appointed ahead of me as well. This was difficult to understand.

Some friends began to suggest that I might have to consider taking legal action because of the obvious unfairness with which I was being treated. It did not seem reasonable for me not to be appointed to a suitable consultant post, despite having all the necessary training, experience, and qualifications. And in addition, unlike many of my competitors, I had numerous publications in recognised professional journals, as well as having a postgraduate doctorate in medicine (MD) from Glasgow University. What did I yet lack?

When the consultant surgeons I was working with directly as senior registrar could not help any further, I felt I had little choice but to speak to someone in higher authority. The most suitable person to speak to would be the consultant who oversaw postgraduate surgical training in the West of Scotland.

I was extremely concerned in case I had some problem that I was not aware of. Perhaps, I thought, I was not as competent in surgery as I should be, and none of my consultant supervisors were prepared to tell me so. Or was it the case that I did not have supporting references? Or even that my curriculum vitae (CV) was not good enough? Once again, I felt that I did not belong here and was just a foreigner who had no rights, despite whatever I had managed to achieve.

I was pleased to be able to arrange an interview with the consultant in charge of postgraduate training. He told me to come to his office for a confidential chat. He had, as it so happened, served on several appointment committees that had interviewed me for consultant posts. I thought he should have good insight into why I was being unsuccessful.

When the day came for the interview, he asked me to come into his office, shut the door, and have a seat. He then, to my surprise, said that what he was about to say to me he could not repeat in public. He then told me that I should have no concerns about what my referees were writing about me. Your references, he said, "would see you into heaven!" As far as my CV was concerned, it was one of the best he had seen for a long time. There were also no difficulties whatsoever with my clinical skills. I was a well-trained and gifted surgeon.

So why, I asked, if I was a well-trained and competent surgeon, was I turned down for every consultant post that I had been interviewed for in the past two years?

The answer he gave me was very surprising. He said that, unlike training posts, a consultant post was "for life", so to speak. Hence, the consultants in the hospital, who were already in post, had the final say as to who was to be appointed. He went on to inform me that the only reason I was not being appointed was simply, "because of the colour of your skin". He was sorry to tell me that. But to encourage me, he said that something similar had happened to him some twenty years earlier. He too had faced similar prejudice because he was of Jewish origin. His advice was not to give up but to just keep going!

I left that meeting, in some way, quite content! It was now clear that I was able and competent enough to take up the post of consultant surgeon after all. But, of course, I could do nothing about my racial origin. I decided that I would not take any legal action against anyone but, as advised, would not stop applying for a consultant post either. I would leave everything in God's hands.

I was, however, somewhat surprised and sad to learn how many intelligent and well-educated senior consultants held such narrow-minded views. This explained to me another phenomenon, which was now no longer surprising—why, like women in surgical practise, consultants from ethnic minorities were always underrepresented in gaining merit awards, as many published studies had pointed out. I was learning through this experience that, whilst education is a wonderful thing, it did not by itself convert "devils into angels" but merely made "devils into clever devils".

Shortly after this helpful meeting, the consultant in charge of postgraduate training phoned and asked me to take on a locum consultant post in Ayrshire. This meant working as a consultant but only for limited period. I was pleased to do this, as it would be good experience. But, in addition, I was informed by the consultant in charge of training that there was to be a retirement of a consultant surgeon in that hospital, and the locum post would set me up very nicely to obtain the permanent post. This sounded very positive, and I willingly agreed to take on the locum post.

Having agreed to take on the post, the very next day, quite unexpectedly, I received another phone call. This was from a consultant surgeon in Dunfermline. He indicated that, whilst he did not know me personally, he was aware that I was the most experienced senior registrar in Scotland. He was looking for someone who was suitably trained to take on the post of locum consultant surgeon to help at his hospital. He went on to tell me that they expected to be able to advertise for a permanent post at the hospital in about nine months' time. The reason for this was that one of their consultants was not well and was thinking of taking early retirement from surgery.

I told the consultant that I had already agreed to take on a locum consultant post in Ayrshire; having given my word, I could not go back on it. I was therefore sorry that I could not help them on this occasion. Then I said something that seemed to come from somewhere in my head. I said to the consultant: "If, however, God wants me to come to Dunfermline, he will alter circumstances and make it happen, and I will come to Dunfermline."

The person on the other side of the phone said that this was very interesting, and we ended the conversation!

On my return home, I told my wife about what had happened that day. You will not be surprised to know that she was not at all happy with my response to the consultant from Dunfermline. She thought I was making things even worse for myself, as people would think that I was a "religious nut" or something worse. After all, I always included the fact that I was a follower of Jesus Christ in my curriculum vitae; surely that was more than enough!

I did my locum consultant post in Ayrshire as planned. Everything seemed to go well, and some local consultants even went as far as to say that they expected me to be working there on a permanent basis soon. The permanent post was soon advertised. And, as expected, I was on the short list for the permanent post. Once again, I was "second" and was not offered the permanent post. This failure made me feel that I was only a foreigner and a stranger and did not really belong here!

Shortly after this failed interview, I was visiting my consultant surgeon friend in Yorkshire—the one whose father had prayed for us when we were both registrars. He had been appointed consultant surgeon two years before me. He happened to be looking through the current *British Medical Journal* in which consultant surgeon posts are advertised. He said to me, "Riaz, I think this is a post for you. It is a general surgical / gastrointestinal post in Dunfermline, Fife."

I could not believe it. I said that I'd been told there would be a post when the current surgeon took early retirement but that this would be in about nine months' time. To my utter surprise, the post had been advertised many months earlier than expected.

After going home and making some enquiries, I was told that the consultant, whose post had become available, had, indeed, decided to retire many months earlier than planned and that I was, of course, very welcome to apply for the post.

On investigating matters further, I found it very interesting to note that the website of the Fife Health Board, which was responsible for advertising the post, had on its letterhead a cross with the words, "health for a kingdom", written across it. This looked very religious to me, but it was open to various interpretations I suppose!

I had no other choice but to apply for the post and was pleased to be included in the group for interview. It soon became clear that the post was very much under the influence of Edinburgh surgeons. The post was clearly an East Coast of Scotland post, and the appointment of someone trained in the West Coast of Scotland was extremely unlikely.

On the appointment committee, in addition to consultants working in Fife, there were two professors from Edinburgh. In addition to me, there were three excellent candidates for the post—who were all trained in Edinburgh. I felt that, as the only outside candidate for the post, especially one trained in Glasgow, I had little chance of being appointed! Still, I had no choice but to do my best and give honest answers to questions asked at the interview. I finished the interview thinking that there would be no chance of me being appointed.

In those days, after being interviewed, all candidates were expected to wait outside the interview room until the committee decided which candidate was to be offered the post. Once that decision was made, the administrator would then come outside the room and invite the successful candidate to come into the interview room to be offered the post. Only then would the other candidates leave!

After the interview, the four of us waited for at least two hours whilst the committee argued as to who should be appointed! We all thought it must be one of the three Edinburgh candidates who would be appointed, and, as they were all excellent, it must be proving difficult for the committee to decide who would be best for the post. Hence, the time taken for them to make up their minds!

Finally, the lady administrator came out of the interview room and, to everyone's surprise, asked me to come into the room. When I sat down, the chairman informed me that the committee, after thorough discussion, had come to a "unanimous" decision that I should be offered the post.

That was a complete surprise. I, of course, accepted the offer, unexpected as it was. I did not have much of a choice anyway! This was the first time I had been offered a consultant post, and I could not refuse it.

Having verbally accepted the post, I was approached by the chairman who told me that he could not believe what was happening! He went on to say that, like me, he was also a Christian, and he knew the other two consultant surgeons I would be working directly with were both Christians as well. In another word, he said that Dunfermline would have three consultant surgeons who were all believers and followers of Jesus Christ. He had never come across such a situation as this before! He seemed to be more amazed and delighted at the outcome than I was.

When I had finished my training some years before, I had asked the Lord to give me the privilege of having one Christian consultant colleague to work with. Now the Lord, in His providence, which no human being can fully comprehend, had given me not one but two Christian colleagues to work with. One of them, it turned out, was the person who had phoned me earlier to ask if I was available to do a locum for them.

Later, as often happens, I got some more information as to the discussions that had taken place at the appointment committee. At the committee meeting, before even seeing any of the four candidates for the post, one of the professors from Edinburgh had asked the local consultants which of the four candidates they wanted. He was surprised to receive the response that they did not yet know. They simply had made up their minds that the best candidate for the post would be chosen. The professors from Edinburgh then did their best to ensure one of their three trainees was offered the post—which was the cause of the two-hour delay in deciding who to call into the interview room.

Apparently, after much argument and debate led by the Edinburgh professors, the final decision made was, indeed, unanimous. In the end, all agreed that I was the best candidate by far and should be offered the post, even though I had been trained in Glasgow!

CHAPTER 11

Experiences as a Consultant Surgeon

I had a wonderful time as a consultant surgeon in the Kingdom of Fife based in Dunfermline. We had to move to Fife, as the rules indicated that a consultant surgeon had to live within a ten-mile radius of the main hospital. I served as a consultant from 1988 to 2001. It was a wonderful privilege indeed to work with two consultant surgical colleagues who were Christians. Whilst we did not always agree on everything, nevertheless, we all fully supported and assisted each other to our benefit and to the benefit of all our patients.

On starting my consultant post, I recall speaking to one of the senior orthopaedic surgeons, who congratulated me on my appointment. He also worked in the same hospital as me. I told him that I'd been informed at the interview that Fife Health Board would be building a brand-new hospital in a couple of years' time, and that was a very exciting prospect for me. He replied that he'd been told the same story some twenty years earlier when he was appointed, but nothing had happened! However, despite that comment, a brand-new hospital was, in fact, built as indicated to me at the interview.

I had the privilege of being present and meeting Princess Anne, the queen's daughter, when she came to declare the hospital open. Our brand-new hospital, known as the Queen Margaret Hospital, was at that time the most modern and best-equipped hospital in Scotland.

After several years working as a consultant surgeon in Fife, I was appointed clinical director, responsible for the management of all surgical services in West Fife and then later for all of Fife. It was a privilege to serve in this capacity. The chief executive appointed to Fife Health Board at that time turned out to be a Christian, as was my business manager. Happy days!

As clinical director for surgery, I discovered that Fife Health Board had the largest waiting list for surgery in the whole of Scotland. This apparently had been the case for a long time. The chief executive and I discussed how this could be corrected.

It was obvious that we needed to do more operations to bring the waiting list down. There were no extra beds or operating theatre time to do the necessary additional work in Fife itself. The solution to the problem required something to be done that had not been done before. The answer lay in operating elsewhere. This had to be in the private sector, as there was no other NHS option.

After some enquiries by the chief executive, it became clear that we could offer Fife patients on all consultant surgeons' waiting lists the opportunity to have their operation done sooner in a private hospital in nearby Stirling. The operations would be done as agreed by me and my consultant surgical colleagues who worked with me in Dunfermline. We would do all operations without charging any private fees for doing so. This had never happened before. Because of the agreement by us not to charge for doing the operations in the private sector, the cost would be very little more than NHS costs. This reminded me of the time when I operated on a Friday afternoon as senior registrar in Glasgow to bring down the waiting list of my consultant supervisor.

Our agreed solution to the long-standing waiting list problem worked extremely well. The patients who had been waiting a long time were offered the opportunity to have their operations done in Stirling. We were delighted when many patients indicated that they would be content to be treated in the private hospital. Soon, Fife had one of the shortest waiting lists for elective procedures in the whole of Scotland!

In addition to long waiting lists, we also had difficulty in treating patients with complicated urgent problems over the winter months. This was not uncommon for other health boards in Scotland.

On one winter, I had to cancel the operation of an older lady with oesophageal cancer twice, as no intensive care bed, which she would require in the post-operative period, was available in the whole of Scotland. It was a very busy time. What to do? It would not be right for the patient, with this extremely dangerous cancer, to have her operation cancelled again, and yet an ITU bed was essential for safe post-operative care. What could be done to solve the problem?

Given our experience with the elective operations in the private sector, the chief executive and I decided the best thing to do would be for the patient to be transferred to a well-known private hospital called the Jubilee Hospital in Clydebank where ITU beds were available. I would have to drive down to the hospital with my registrar and operate on my patient there. She would then be transferred back to Dunfermline by ambulance a few days after the operation when an ITU bed was no longer required. This worked out very well. The patient spent four days in ITU and then was safely transferred back to Fife. Whilst obviously not ideal, it at least got the operation done safely. Given the success of this operation, my consultant colleagues who also had patients needing ITU beds asked for permission to do the same with their patients. This worked for their patients too. As no private fees were charged by any of us, the problem was solved in our patients' best interests, with no significant additional cost to the NHS.

One day, totally unexpectedly, I received a letter inviting me to attend number 10 Downing Street in London, as a representative of Fife Health Board, to meet with then UK Prime Minister Mr Tony Blair. Janet and I made our way to London, though only I could attend the meeting. She, of course, had to be there to ensure that I was correctly dressed for the occasion!

It was very interesting to see inside the official home of the prime minister. I recall walking up stairs to get to the official meeting room. I noted that there were photographs of all the past prime ministers on the wall. Interestingly, they were all in black and white.

When Mr Blair arrived for the meeting, he was shown round various well-known professors, who tried to spend as much time with him as possible. I got the impression that we, the "ordinary invitees", would not get a chance to speak with Mr Blair directly. He was being chaperoned very carefully indeed.

As time began to ebb, I noticed that Mr Blair seemed to say that he wanted some time on his own. The professors all stepped back. It was then I saw him approaching the small group of people who were standing with me. He came over and needlessly introduced himself as Mr Blair. He asked me then what NHS sector I was representing.

When I told him that I was from Dunfermline in Fife, he immediately said, "Ah yes, that's Gordon Brown, the chancellor's territory."

He then asked me for my thoughts on how the National Health Service could be improved.

I suggested that the best thing for government to do was to take the National Health Service out of politics all together. How could this be done? was his question. I replied that this could be done by his government appointing a multiparty committee, who would then follow advice from recognised experts in the field and come up with a rolling ten-year plan for the NHS. This plan would then be followed—no matter which party was in power.

Whilst Mr Blair thought this was worth considering, I regret to say, this did not ever happen. Will it happen one day? Who knows!

After the meeting was over and we all left number 10 Downing Street, I met up with my wife, who wanted to know how things had gone. I told her what had happened at the meeting and then said I was feeling a little hungry, as I hadn't gotten much to eat at the meeting. Given the lateness of the night, we went to a local McDonald's for a burger. This ensured I did not get carried away with pomposity in any way!

On another occasion, Janet and I also had the privilege of meeting Her Majesty the Queen in Holyrood Palace, in Edinburgh. As representative of Fife Health Board, I was invited to attend with my wife a Royal garden party. That also was an honour and a privilege indeed. We had a wonderful day.

It just so happened, as things do, that we met up with a family from our previous church, who were also invited to the Royal garden party. The daughter of the couple, well known to us, suffered from Down's syndrome but was quite good at horse riding. As the gentleman who walked ahead of the queen deciding to whom Her Majesty could speak, as obviously, she could not speak personally to everyone, I stepped forward and suggested Her Majesty may be interested in speaking to our Down's syndrome friend, as she was involved with horse riding. To my surprise, this suggestion was accepted. So, when Her Majesty came to where we were, she stopped to speak to our friends. This did mean that we were very close to Her Majesty and saw her clearly discussing her interest in horse riding. It was a privilege indeed to be invited to such a wonderful occasion.

As a Christian believer, I thought that I needed to do something "religious" in relation to my faith in the hospital where I worked. I started a prayer meeting in my office in Dunfermline, for any doctor who wished to attend to pray for our patients. Both my consultant colleagues, as well as others, attended on a regular basis. We had some wonderful times praying for our patients and seeing some excellent results. I suspect this would not have happened in any of the other consultant posts that I had failed to get. The Lord knows best!

Many patients I came across over the years as a consultant would never be forgotten by me. I remember one senior local lawyer who came to me with a surgical problem. He could, of course, have gone to a private hospital for treatment in Edinburgh, but he chose to come to my unit.

After successful treatment, he sent a present to my home as a way of thanking me for my work. It turned out to be a crate of the best champagne sent all the way from France. I did not drink alcohol much, but my wife thoroughly enjoyed the present.

I also had the privilege of operating on a local well-known Member of Parliament, who decided to come to me for treatment. I was able to give him a date for his operation that was suitable for him in relation to his duties at the House of Parliament in London.

All went well, but before he was discharged, I was asked to see someone who wanted to thank me personally for my treatment of the MP. It turned out to be none other than the current Secretary of State for Scotland!

Sadly, not all patients were treated successfully. I remember operating on an elderly Church of Scotland minister who I had met many years before at the 428 Club in Glasgow. He was now retired and lived in Dunfermline. He had developed cancer of the oesophagus. The surgical treatment of this cancer had become my main interest by this time, and I was operating on all patients with this deadly diagnosis in Fife. Before my appointment, all such patients had to be sent to Edinburgh for surgical treatment. We, of course, knew each other, and it was my responsibility and privilege to operate on this church minister.

The operation went technically well, and he seemed to make a good early recovery. Sadly, the recovery did not last long, as he developed post-operative pneumonia. Despite all treatment, his condition deteriorated rapidly.

As I was speaking to him one morning, he took hold of my hand and said to me, "Riaz, I'm ready! I'm ready."

I knew exactly what he meant.

Later that week, sadly he passed away.

It was my privilege, on invitation from the family, to read a passage of the Bible at his funeral. Before doing so, I indicated to those who attended the funeral that he had told me that, "he was 'ready'". I added that, as a minister of the gospel, he would, I am sure, ask them to consider whether they were ready to pass on from this life too.

I always considered keeping up to date with developments in surgery of extreme importance. In order to do so, I attended a seminar in London where a surgeon from the United States was invited to speak. He told the audience about performing a new operation using what is now commonly called "key-hole" surgery, to remove diseased gallbladders for gallstones. Removing the gallbladder was one of the most common operations in the Western world. And after an open operation to do the procedure, patients often stayed in hospital for over a week to recover sufficiently before being allowed to go home.

With "key-hole" surgery, if performed properly, patients would not only have much smaller scars but would also recover more quickly than by the standard operation. This would be best for patients, and in addition, as patients would be able to go home much sooner, this would reduce the cost of the procedure for the NHS.

I decided to learn how to perform this new procedure. At that time, the only way to do this was to do the operation on anaesthetised animals. I therefore had to attend suitable training courses in Dublin and then in France, where this was legally allowed. Having done so, I was ready to perform the procedure on patients back home in Dunfermline.

By good fortune, a drug representative of the company that was making the necessary equipment for key-hole surgery lived in Dunfermline and was very keen for me to borrow the equipment to perform this operation. By this time, the operation had only been performed in professorial units in Edinburgh and Dundee. So, we would be the third hospital in Scotland to perform this procedure.

We set up the equipment, and in order to let the theatre nursing staff know how things should be done, I performed a procedure using a large cardboard box to act as the abdomen of a patient and a balloon filled with water to represent the gallbladder. Then, using the borrowed equipment, the balloon was extracted from the cardboard box. This gave the nurses, who had never seen this done before, a good idea of what a patient undergoing this procedure would require. Having done this, the theatre nurses were now ready and eager to do this procedure on a real patient. But who would volunteer to be the first patient for this new operation?

The next day, a young lady came in for a standard gallbladder operation. I spoke to her and informed her about the new procedure that was becoming available and wondered if she would consider being the first person in Fife to undergo this operation. I informed her that, if she agreed to have the operation by this new method, she would be the first human I would have performed the operation on. There was no pressure on her, as obviously, we would do the operation by the standard fashion if she preferred.

To my utter amazement, this young lady said immediately that she would be happy to consent to the procedure and that "someone has to be the first!" I was overcome by her courage and humanity. What a lady!

The operation was performed as arranged the next morning. It was great to do this procedure successfully with no complications. When the gallbladder came out of the patient, to my astonishment, everyone in theatre began to clap. This was the first time ever that I had such a reaction!

The lady recovered extremely well. She wanted to go home the next day! However, just to make sure there were no complications, we made her stay in hospital for three days. Finally, we had to let her go home. Apparently, that very day she went shopping. I am not sure how this happened, but she was spotted by the local press and her picture and story appeared in the local newspapers. Not surprisingly, the question was raised as to why more patients were not receiving this type of surgery!

Sadly, there were considerable issues raised by some managers about the cost of buying new equipment for this type of surgery. Some thought there was little point in spending so much money on new equipment for surgery that should only be done in large centres such as the Professorial Surgical Unit in Edinburgh. I took the view that it was much more likely that this type of operation would become the "standard operation" in all surgical units. Some also refused to accept the argument that key-hole surgery would save money, in that patients would recover much more quickly than by the traditional open operation and would, hence, go home earlier.

Despite these reasonable arguments for purchasing the necessary equipment, the management refused to do so. Furthermore, I was criticised for bringing the matter to the attention of the local press. This accusation was simply derogatory and wrong. I had to make it clear that I would take legal action if that accusation were passed around. After all, giving such information to the public would be breaking patient confidentiality and doing such a thing would make a guilty doctor open to legal action by the General Medical Council. I would never break patient confidentiality, and hence, taking a strong position against some managers was my only option. Fortunately, the matter went no further.

It so happened that it was around this time that the old surgical hospital in Dunfermline, called the Dunfermline and West Fife Hospital, was closing and the new hospital to be known as the Queen Margaret Hospital was taking its place.

Given the publicity that the first patient undergoing "key-hole" surgery in Fife had generated, it turned out that some ladies from the rotary club from the "old hospital" became interested in purchasing equipment as a gift for the "new hospital". In a very short time, they managed to gather enough money to purchase the necessary equipment, thus making it possible for key-hole surgery service to commence at the opening of the new hospital.

As a way of saying thanks for the gift to those who had contributed financially, I decided to make a video of an actual operation carried out with the equipment gifted. That, together with the equipment itself, was made available for people to see at an "open to the public Saturday" in the new hospital. To everyone's surprise, on that Saturday, many people came to the open day, which turned out to a very busy but very interesting day indeed.

Was it because of this incident and how it was handled by me that I was later appointed clinical director for surgery and became part of the new surgical management team in our new hospital? I don't know. However, it was without doubt the best development for patients with gallbladder disease. It meant that patients from Fife did not need to travel to Edinburgh or Dundee for this operation. Furthermore, in time, I helped my fellow surgical colleagues learn to perform key-hole surgery as well, to the benefit of all our patients.

One summer, whilst we were on a family holiday in Corfu, I came across a couple who joined our Christian holiday group for a few days. Discussion with them resulted in me finding out that they had been working as missionaries in Eastern Europe, helping the poor to start small businesses. Unfortunately, the lady was suffering a great deal of pain from gallbladder disease and needed to have her gallbladder removed as soon as possible. They were due to go back to the United States for the operation. There was, however, a great deal of concern on their part because of the expense for such an operation, as they had no health insurance.

In our conversation, I discovered that they were due to come to Motherwell in Scotland for a short visit. I informed them that Motherwell was near enough to Dunfermline for her to consider coming to Dunfermline for her necessary operation. I advised them that, not only was I a consultant surgeon working in Dunfermline, I was also able to perform the gallbladder surgery she needed.

In addition, they were welcome to stay in our home, and I would seek necessary permission from our management to perform the procedure and would be happy to pay for any necessary cost. They could not believe it. God had indeed answered their prayers!

In due course, they came to Scotland. After fulfilling their commitments in Motherwell, they came over to Dunfermline. I managed to take out her gallbladder through "key-hole" surgery on my Thursday operating day. She recovered well and was out shopping on Saturday, and they both flew to the United States on Sunday. She had no complications and recovered completely.

I was fortunate enough to meet up with her husband many years later when he happened to be visiting the United Kingdom and had a speaking engagement at a church in Glasgow. He told me that his wife was keeping very well and that he had often spoken of the way God had worked in their life following our meeting on holiday in Corfu.

One night whilst on call, I had a very "interesting case" to deal with as an emergency! It concerned a young man who was out celebrating his birthday. He'd had some alcohol to drink and was walking about in his mother's garden. He'd slipped and fallen heavily on his side, landing on a metal rod.

This metal rod penetrated his right armpit and then went over his collarbone into the right side of his neck and came out on the left side of his neck. It was a miracle that he was still alive when he was brought to casualty. My registrar phoned me that night and asked me to come into casualty right away.

He'd had an X-ray done, which showed the metal rod in relationship to his spine. It had penetrated the neck between the spine and the gullet and must have been very close to the major blood vessels in the neck. If any one of the major blood vessels started to bleed, the chances of him surviving were very small indeed.

I took him straight to theatre with all the support staff present and ready to go. The consultant anaesthetist on emergency duty arranged for a bed to be made available in the intensive care unit, just in case he survived his surgery!

As often was the case, I prayed to the Lord for help and then got on with the operation. I decided that, if anything major, such as the common carotid artery, had been damaged, he would have been dead by now. Also, if he was very fortunate and all the major blood vessels had not been damaged, I would need to be very careful when removing the rod. I did not want to make matters worse.

So, after careful thought, I sterilised the metal staff and then pulled it out in exactly the same pathway that it had gone in. It was just fantastic to note that he was stable, with no evidence of major bleeding after removal of the metal rod! I then cleaned the wound in the right armpit and that on the left side of his neck and simply stitched both up. That was the end of the operation. The patient went to ITU and did very well overnight. He recovered completely! He was the luckiest person alive.

As this patient turned out to be a professional actor, he reported matters to the press, and soon there was tremendous interest about his case from all over the world. Several film crews came from the United Kingdom, Europe, and America to document this incident. I, therefore, gave them the surgical perspective and said I felt it was a genuine miracle for this young man to escape such an accident with only two small wounds to show for it.

This case was rare and interesting enough to be published in the *British Medical Journal*. In addition, I was asked to play my part as the surgeon on the night he came in as an emergency in order to make a short film of the incident. This film was then shown throughout the Western world on television and still appears on an occasion as a short "filler" film from time to time.

It amazed me that this one-off case, which in the end of the day needed very little input from me and my team, gave us more publicity than any other case I had played any part in!

Another part of my duty as an experienced consultant surgeon was that I became a representative for Fife on the list of consultants who acted as external assessors for the appointment of new consultants throughout Scotland. Having come through a difficult situation myself in the past, in that my appointment to a consultant position was unnecessarily delayed for wrong reasons, I did my best to ensure that all interviews were done properly and justly so that the best candidate was appointed on my watch.

I also became an examiner for the Fellowship Examinations of the Royal College of Surgeons and Physicians of Glasgow. For the clinical examination to be properly conducted, suitable patients had to be asked for their permission to take part in such examinations. I had no difficulty in obtaining necessary consent from many of my patients in Fife.

On one occasion, an external examiner came to examine with me. He was a professor of surgery in Lahore, Pakistan. We got on quite well, and he was very impressed with the set-up for the examination. Afterwards, he said to me that I should be given an honorary professorship from the College of Surgeons of Pakistan. In addition, I should be coming regularly to Pakistan to lecture to students and doctors there. He said that he would like to make the arrangements for this to happen and would like me to send him a copy of my CV so that he could take things forward.

I must confess that I did not take this invitation very seriously and, at first, took no action. To my surprise, some two weeks later, my secretary received a phone call from the professor saying that he had not yet received a copy of my CV; he would be grateful if she could forward a copy to him as soon as possible.

I was left with little choice, as I did not wish to be impolite. I had to send him a copy of my CV. There was, however, one matter that did cause me a little concern. It was this. I had always indicated in my CV that, despite my name, I was a Christian and followed Jesus Christ as my Lord and Saviour. The question that came to my mind was whether or not to take out this information. After all, the information would be in the hands of Muslim believers who may not appreciate this confession of faith.

I naturally spoke to several colleagues about the matter and most felt that, given the opportunity offered, I should compromise and simply take out the paragraph about my Christian position listed under "outside interests".

After a great deal of thought and prayer, I concluded that I should not remove this information, and hence, my CV was sent to the professor in its original form. I heard nothing further from the Professor.

Later that week, the Royal College held a dinner, as was customary for all its examiner consultants. I was, as usual, invited to attend.

At that dinner, I saw the professor, who was also attending. Perhaps, not unexpectedly, he kept himself away from me, remaining on the other side of the college hall and making every attempt to ignore me. I received no further communications from him. As a Christian believer, I had become a foreigner and a stranger even to those of the same ethnicity and born in the same country as me!

One day at home, as I was eating dinner, I found myself in terrible pain. My wife thought I was having a heart attack, but I reassured her that that was not the case. I was having pain from my gallbladder!

Further tests showed that I did, indeed, have gallstones in an inflamed gallbladder and needed to have an operation to remove it. The question then arose, where to have this operation done?

It was "traditional" for consultants in my position, who lived and worked in Dunfermline, to have any necessary operation done either privately or have the operation done in a large teaching hospital in Edinburgh. Neither of these two options appealed to me. I felt that, as I lived in Fife, I should be treated in Fife like everyone else. If the Fife NHS service was good enough for my patients, then it was good enough for me.

I spoke to my consultant surgeon colleagues and asked if they would be prepared to operate on me. They were not very keen to do so. When I asked them why they felt that way, they said that, usually, I would be expected to go to Edinburgh for such an operation.

I suggested that I had complete trust in their ability. Also, I had been responsible for helping to teach them how to do "key-hole" surgery for gallbladder disease. Hence, I was sure they knew how to do it properly. They were operating on other patients with gallbladder disease, and I felt that there was no good reason why they could operate on me as well.

My consultant colleagues said that they would like to think about this for a day or so to decide what to do.

Eventually, my two consultant colleagues, who were both Christians, decided that the two of them would do the operation on me together.

Also, I wanted to be nursed in my own ward, as I knew the calibre of my ward's nursing staff and felt sure I would be well looked after.

Things went well for me, and there were no complications from the operation. The main thing, however, was the interesting fact that the nursing staff were delighted and felt honoured that a consultant surgeon of my standing was prepared to come to their ward to be nursed by them. I could not understand that. I felt that I was the one being honoured by them for their courtesy and kindness in looking after me so well.

CHAPTER 12

Time of Change

After living and serving for about thirteen years very happily and successfully in Fife as consultant surgeon, I noticed that my wife was becoming somewhat restless. Janet began to think that it was time to move! Both our children had left Fife to study law at Aberdeen University, and she began to feel that it was time to go back to Glasgow!

I, of course, could not fully understand why she felt like this and had difficulty taking it in. We were both happy in Dunfermline, and I was certainly very content in my career, which was progressing extremely well. After all, I was now a senior consultant and clinical director for Fife, as well as being on the Scottish committee for appointing consultants in Scotland. In addition, I had the privilege of being offered the surgical fellowship without examination by the Edinburgh College of Surgeons. What could be better? What would be the logical reason for giving all this up and moving away? Whilst she could not give an answer to every question I had in mind, Janet still felt that something was about to happen, and we would be better off back in Glasgow! I did not understand at that time that God was moving ahead in our best interests.

Just at this time in my surgical speciality, a Scotland-wide study of the outcome of patients undergoing surgery for cancer of the oesophagus showed that this was a very difficult cancer to deal with. The opinion of the professor who carried out the study was that patients with oesophageal cancer should only be treated in major teaching hospitals with at least two consultants available to specialise in this extremely difficult to treat condition.

This study gave me a potential problem. I was now, in fact, specialising in the surgical treatment of oesophageal cancer in Fife, and the outcome data of my patients showed that my results were as good as any other specialist in Scotland. However, I was the only surgeon in Fife doing this kind of surgery. And as things were changing, I would have to consider a potential move to a teaching hospital, perhaps in Edinburgh or Glasgow, or possibly consider giving up oesophageal surgery altogether!

Whilst I was considering these things, as well as working hard in Fife, I noticed an advert for a consultant surgeon post in a teaching hospital called the Victoria Infirmary in Glasgow. The hospital was looking for an experienced senior consultant who would, in time, take over the leadership of upper gastrointestinal surgery for the South Glasgow University Hospitals Trust.

This certainly seemed to be a reasonable next step up for me in clinical surgery, but it did mean leaving Fife and going back to a teaching hospital in Glasgow. This was, of course, on the assumption that I would be appointed to such a post! Having been unsuccessful in obtaining a consultant post in the West of Scotland previously, I felt there was no guarantee I would be successful now!

As often is the case, it was difficult to ignore my wife's concerns about moving from Fife! Why would she start thinking about going back to Glasgow just before a very suitable senior post became available? Was the Lord moving in some way?

I felt that I had no choice. The least I could do was to make some enquiries concerning this post. I phoned the appropriate department to make an initial enquiry. On doing so, I got through to a lady in the administration department who was responsible for arranging everything for this post. She told me immediately, that she was sorry, but the post had been withdrawn! Being a Glaswegian lass, she was very open! She told me that the reason for the withdrawal of the post was that there had arisen a dispute between the two main hospitals of the South Glasgow Health Board. The Victoria Hospital consultants wanted an upper gastrointestinal surgeon, as advertised, but the other hospital consultants, who worked in the Southern General Hospital, wanted a colorectal surgeon instead. As an agreement could not be reached, management had decided that the advertised post should simply be withdrawn.

When I told my wife this, she was deeply disappointed, as she was sure this was the way forward for us. But she accepted that we had no choice but to continue working and living in Fife.

A short time later, totally unexpectedly, the post was re-advertised. This was very unusual, even for the National Health Service! I had to make another phone call to find out what was happening.

When I phoned, I got the same lady on the phone who I'd spoken with previously. She told me that the disagreement between the two hospitals had been resolved. The Victoria Infirmary consultants had won. Hence, the upper gastrointestinal consultant surgical post, very suitable for me, was back on the market.

My wife was delighted to see the advert, and I had by now little choice but to apply. There was, of course, no guarantee I would make the short list—never mind get the post itself. Also, the application form made it clear that, if an applicant did not make the short list and consequently did not hear from the trust within four weeks, he could assume that his application was not successful. This would save the cost of any further postage! This seemed clear enough.

It just so happened that, at this time, I was about to lead a team of doctors to France on behalf of Fife Health Board for a conference about day surgery. The timing of this conference could collide with a possible interview date for the post at the Victoria Infirmary. Naturally, I informed the Glasgow Health Board about this possibility in a cover note sent with my application form.

I went off to France with my team as originally planned. My wife and I had decided that we would keep in touch, and, if need be, I would get a flight back to Glasgow for the interview. It was best not to cancel this important visit to France, and it would help to keep things confidential concerning any possible move to Glasgow.

We had a good and useful conference in France, but whilst I was away, there came no word from the Victoria Infirmary! So, when I came home, it seemed quite clear that the lack of communication meant I was not on the short list for the post. I was not all that surprised and not too bothered about it. Janet was very disappointed. She did, however, accept that we would just have to continue with our life in Fife whilst awaiting some other opportunity for change in the future.

A week after my return from France, I was in my outpatient clinic in Dunfermline when the outpatient sister informed me there was a telephone call for me from Glasgow. This was very unusual. I did not often get phone calls during my outpatient clinics. On answering the phone call, I found myself speaking to the same administrator lady from Glasgow, yet again!

To my utter surprise, she asked me when I would be free to come for an interview for the consultant post at the Victoria Infirmary! She went on to explain that, as I was going to be in France according to the information I had submitted with my application, it was decided by the board to cancel the planed interviews and reschedule them at a time when I would be available. She was asking me now when I would be free so that the interviews could take place!

I, therefore, looked at my diary and suggested a possible date and time when I would be free to attend for an interview. I'd never before had this kind of experience in obtaining a consultant post! What was going on?

Whilst I was waiting for the interviews to take place, I had an international surgical examination to assist at, as one of the surgical examiners for the Royal College of Surgeons and Physicians of Glasgow. I had to go with the examination team to Abu Dhabi to conduct examinations there. As I was thinking about how best to get there, I received a phone call from a consultant friend who was also on the examination team of the college. He was a consultant surgeon in Stirling, not far from Dunfermline. He suggested that perhaps he and I could make our way to Heathrow Airport from Edinburgh Airport to save us having to go to Glasgow Airport. This would be more convenient for us both. I agreed, and so we both left from Edinburgh Airport.

As I sat with my consultant colleague on the aeroplane, we began to speak about family life, work, the future, and such things. I then felt the need to share with him the fact that I had applied for a consultant post in Glasgow. I thought that, if I did not say what was going on in my surgical career, it would seem very impolite when the information became public, as it was sure to do. So, I decided just to tell him and ask him to keep it confidential. After all, there was no guarantee that I would be appointed to this senior post anyway!

To my great surprise, on hearing that I had applied for the post, he simply said, "I know." He went on to elaborate. He was, in fact, the external consultant on the appointment committee for the post! He was told that the first date for the interview had been cancelled and that another date would soon be issued. He obviously knew which consultants had applied for this post and took the view that I was highly favoured for the post. I suggested that, given his position on the appointment committee, I was happy not to discuss the matter any further, so as not to cause him any embarrassment. He agreed that was the best thing to do. I was, however, glad that I mentioned my interest in the post to him.

It also happened that one of the other examiners on the team was a senior breast surgeon who also worked in the Victoria Infirmary. I decided that it would be best for me not to mention my interest in the post. This would save any possible conflict or, indeed, embarrassment for him. So, we did not mention anything about the post to each other for several days.

Then on one evening, the examiners' group was invited out on to a Sultan's boat. It was a beautiful warm evening. The stars were shining very brightly in the darkness of the night. We all had a great time laughing and joking together. At the end of the evening, there was even greater excitement! Someone shouted excitedly that the belly dancers were coming on board!

I was not all that interested in that type of dance, and at that point, the consultant from the Victoria Infirmary, who also was not too keen to see the dancing, asked if he and I could have some food just sitting on the deck under the stars. That was just right for me, and so I agreed.

As we sat there eating, he turned to me and said that he was very much in favour of me being appointed consultant to the Victoria Infirmary. It was his view that they could do with someone with my ability, experience, and expertise in upper gastrointestinal surgery. I was somewhat surprised to hear him say that. I told him that the reason I had not raised the issue of my application for this consultant post was that I did not want to cause any embarrassment to him, given that I knew he was a senior consultant at the Victoria Infirmary and may well have a say as to who should be appointed. I was, however, really interested in the post, as it seemed to be the best way forward in my career.

The reason I told him I was genuinely interested in being appointed was that some consultants were seeking other consultant posts not because they wanted to move from their current position but to seek better conditions from their current employer by giving the threat of a possible move to another post. He told me that he fully understood my position, and he knew that I would not be the kind of person who would act in this unethical way. He genuinely wanted me to be appointed to the post. I found this very encouraging indeed.

A week after I'd returned home, I had the interview for the job as planned. The interview seemed to go well. After the interview, I was informed that I would be phoned with the result on my mobile and that I did not have to wait to hear the outcome. This was extremely convenient for me. I was taking my son, Mark, from Dunfermline to Edinburgh, as he had an interview that same afternoon for a trainee post as a lawyer. I was, thus, able to go back home to take my son to Edinburgh for his interview. As I was driving over the Forth Road Bridge into Edinburgh, my mobile phone began to ring. I stopped in a lay-by to take the call.

It was the same lady from administration again! She was phoning to say that I was being offered the post, and she would be obliged if I would give a response. I was able to confirm that I would accept the post but would only resign from my current post in Fife on receiving an appropriate written offer. This seemed reasonable to her and was agreed to.

Janet and I took our son Mark for his interview and then we waited patiently in the car to hear the result. It was difficult to enjoy my new career development, as my son's interview result was an important time in his life and career.

When he came back to the car after his interview, he told us that he too had been successful in obtaining his traineeship. We all had a wonderful and glorious time congratulating each other on our successes. Life was good, praise God!

CHAPTER 13

Sudden Turn for the Worse!

Things seemed to be going very well. I was now simply awaiting written confirmation of my appointment as consultant to the South Glasgow NHS Trust before informing Fife Health Board of my move back to Glasgow. You may not be surprised to read that, when my contract from Glasgow Health Board came through the post, it was incorrect!

I had been given a lower salary than I was due. This was clearly not acceptable. I got in touch with the management to point out the error to them. They agreed that a mistake had been made. I was advised that I should ignore the received contract and that another one would be sent to me right away.

When the new contract came through, it was also wrong! The mistake concerning my salary level had been rectified, but the contract stated that I was to be based at the Southern General Hospital, rather than the Victoria Infirmary.

Once again, the advice was to dispose of the wrong contract and that another one was on the way.

On the third attempt, everything was finally correct! I therefore signed the contract and posted it back to the Glasgow Health Board. I also sent a letter of resignation to Fife Health Board. That was it. We were going back to Glasgow, just as Janet had wanted.

We began the process of our move to Glasgow. I did receive communication from the chairman of Fife Health Board, who informed me that the board members had received my letter of resignation and were very sorry to see me go but fully understood the reasoning behind the move and were very supportive.

On the very day that I signed the correct contract accepting the post in Glasgow, totally out of the blue, I received a phone call from the Occupational Health Consultant of Fife Health Board informing me of a potentially problem that could be very serious!

The situation, he explained, was this. Six months earlier, I had treated an elderly patient who had been an ambulance worker. He'd come in as an emergency patient with an acute gallbladder problem. I'd operated on him and removed his gallbladder, making him much better. He had gone home well. Some months later, I had received a phone call from his general practitioner informing me that this patient had developed jaundice (yellowness of the skin) and was not well. The GP thought that, given that I had removed his gallbladder some months earlier, I must have left some gallstones behind in his bile duct. This is a known complication of gallbladder surgery.

I thought that was not likely, as I was very sure that all the gallstones had been removed and that, at the time of the operation, his bile duct had been clear of stones. Nevertheless, I agreed it would be best for this patient to be admitted to my ward for further investigation and treatment. He came in a few hours later.

When I saw him, it was immediately clear to me that this patient's very severe jaundice was not of "surgical" origin at all. He clearly, to my mind, had a very severe form of jaundice from inflammation of the liver, caused by some viral infection giving rise to what is known as hepatitis. I was sure this was not related to retained gallbladder stones. After discussion with the consultant on call, I had the patient transferred urgently to the infectious diseases unit for further expert management of his non-surgical jaundice.

I was informed later that this patient had, indeed, developed jaundice due to severe hepatitis—later identified as hepatitis B. Sad to say, despite all attempts at treatment, he died of this very severe viral infection. The question then arose as to how, why, and when he had been infected by this virus.

As legally required, external experts were appointed to ensure that a full investigation took place. It is not always easy or possible to trace every source of hepatitis B, but all required procedures needed to be meticulously followed. Despite every effort, the relevant experts were not able to discover how this patient had acquired this deadly infection.

As I had operated on the patient earlier, I was involved in part of the investigation. My occupational health records showed that I had been fully immunised against hepatitis B and had demonstrated the development of adequate antibodies against the virus. Furthermore, I had been given a "certificate for life", confirming that I need not attend again for any further testing or immunisation against hepatitis B. These were the recognised rules.

Given this background, the investigation committee concluded I could not be the source from which the deceased patient had acquired hepatitis B. After a full and complete investigation of all other staff involved, the conclusion reached was that it was not possible to identify the cause of this patient's hepatitis B. The matter was closed.

All this had happened some six months earlier, before the move to Glasgow was even thought about. Now, some hours after signing the Glasgow contract and my resignation letter and posting them both, I was informed that another patient of mine had been diagnosed with hepatitis B. This patient, as is more usually the case, had recovered well. But another investigation to try and identify the source was unavoidable.

The Occupation Health Consultant felt that I could not be the source, as I had been fully investigated already, but he felt that he should inform me in any case, as I was the patient's consultant. I suggested that it might be best for me to undergo some further tests for hepatitis B to ensure that I was not in any way the cause. The consultant thought that my being the source was extremely unlikely and told me there was no legal requirement for me to be tested at this stage.

After some further discussion, I said I would prefer to be tested immediately to ensure that everything was completely covered. If, as expected, I was not involved, other members of my team then could be investigated in the hope that, if possible, a cause could be found.

Reluctantly the occupational health consultant agreed. I had blood tests taken that very day and was advised by the consultant to tell no one that I was undergoing these tests for the sake of confidentiality. The consultant said he expected these tests to be clear. The tests had to be done in a centre in London, as no other centre in the United Kingdom was recognised for legal purposes. He advised further that it would take a couple of weeks for the results to be known. This proved to be a very difficult time for me, as I was saying goodbye to many of my colleagues, who were aware that I was about to leave Fife, but I could not share anything with them about me being tested for hepatitis B.

When the results came back from London, the occupational health consultant was utterly dumbfounded. As it turned out, the results showed that, despite all the immunisation I had received, I had become a carrier of hepatitis B. How long I had been in that position was unknown, and the result was totally unexpected.

These positive results then caused major problems. All my patients had to be informed of the situation and were advised that they could call the hospital on dedicated telephone lines for further advice. Several hundred patients I had treated were tested, and no one was found to have had hepatitis B.

There was also major nationwide publicity. My hepatitis B carrier status was publicised on every television news channel. I was inundated with newspaper reporters congregating outside our house. I had been warned that this might well happen, and I was asked to consider going away somewhere in secret to avoid having to speak to the press.

Whilst I was thinking about doing this, my son Mark told me not to go anywhere. He said that I had done nothing wrong and had no need to hide from the press. He further took out his cricket bat and said, "Don't worry, Dad. I'll make sure no one comes into the house without permission!"

What a boy! I took his advice and stayed at home.

After discussion with my medical defence organisation, it was decided that I should give a statement from my perspective for broadcasting on television. This did have the desired outcome of bringing the media attention on me to an end. However, a problem remained. Despite having been immunised against hepatitis B and having fulfilled all the necessary legal requirements to protect myself and my patients, something totally unexpected had happened. I had become a hepatitis B carrier. Why had this happened?

Some people, as often happens, started to ask all kinds of questions. If I was a hepatitis B carrier how had I acquired the infection? Was I secretly gay? Did I have other infections as well? Whilst not legally required to do so, I gave permission to be tested for other viral infections. These included Hepatitis C and HIV. These results were, as expected, all negative.

No doubt, because of the nationwide publicity and the final outcome in my case, the then Scottish Health minister decided that the current rules and regulations needed to be looked at. Soon, further amendments were instituted to make it safer for patients and reduce the risk of acquiring hepatitis B infection when undergoing surgical procedures. It was also decided that, in the future, anyone entering the medical profession would be tested for hepatitis B surface antigen before being allowed to study medicine. This had not been a requirement in the past. At least, I thought, something positive had resulted from this dreadful experience for me and my family.

Whilst going through this horrendous time, I was overwhelmed by the support I received from many friends, neighbours, and patients. Bouquets of flowers received from many sources, including local churches, filled the house. I could no longer walk down the Dunfermline town centre without being noticed. Many people very kindly would shout words of support and encouragement.

Whilst it was good to have this level of public support, I was now extremely glad we were moving to Glasgow. I thought I would have more anonymity there, which would suit me much better. I could now understand why the lord had arranged for us to move to Glasgow long before the hepatitis B incident was even known about.

However, there were many other hurdles to overcome. The main complicating factor was that I was in the process of moving to a new consultant surgeon's post! What would happen now? Would I be unemployable as a consultant surgeon? What would happen to my newly signed contract? Would the Glasgow Health Board withdraw this contract? Would Fife Health Board consider taking me back? All these questions needed answers to allow me to move on in my life.

A new chief executive had taken over management in Fife, and he made it clear that my problem now lay with the chief executive of the Glasgow Health Board and not with him. I had resigned from my Fife consultant post. So, as far as he was concerned, that was the end of the matter.

The chairman of the Fife Health Board, however, was much more supportive. He made it clear I would not be unemployed whilst he was chairman. This was very kind of him and very encouraging. However, I took the view that leaving Dunfermline for the relative anonymity of Glasgow was in my best interests. In retrospect, God was in control. He had made changes to my circumstances to allow a move to Glasgow some six months before any of the hepatitis B circumstances were even known. God holds the future in His hands.

I had, by this time, sold our home in Fife and had purchased one in Newton Mearns in Glasgow. But we had not yet moved in. Would we be homeless if I did not receive a salary and could not pay the mortgage? What about my own health? Would I also develop jaundice and die of liver failure? These thoughts took over my life for a few weeks. I wondered why God had let this happen. He had the power to prevent all this but had not done so. After all, I had not done anything wrong. I had followed all the legal requirements of United Kingdom law for doctors in order, among other things, not to infect others with hepatitis B. I had been in surgical practise for over twenty-five years without any problems. But for some unknown reason, this had still happened. Life is not always easy!

The first issue to be addressed was whether my contract with the Glasgow Health Board would be honoured. After all, the board had appointed me to operate on patients with oesophageal and gastric cancer. But because of the hepatitis B developments, I would not be allowed to operate on anyone until my liver cleared itself of the virus and I could no longer infect anyone. It was, therefore, a possibility that, as I could no longer fulfil my side of the contract, the contract would be withdrawn. Also, as I had submitted my resignation to the Fife Health Board unilaterally, the current chief executive had made it clear that he would not allow me to withdraw my resignation. In theory, then, I could be unemployed!

I was supported through all this time by my trade union, the British Medical Association. But even they could not guarantee my contract would be honoured. I am glad to say that, despite all these difficulties, all my consultant colleagues from the Victoria Infirmary got in touch with me to assure me of their support and encouraged me to come and get started at the Victoria Infirmary as soon as I could. The operating side of my surgical practise, they said, could simply await events. In the meanwhile, there were plenty of other things for me to do.

As it happened, the Glasgow Health Board, despite the obvious change in my health circumstances, honoured my contract. It was, however, suggested to me by the management that, because of all the stress I'd had to endure, it might be best for me to take a month off work before starting at the Victoria Infirmary.

One of my senior consultant colleagues suggested the opposite. His view was that I should start right away and "get my feet under the table". This seemed the right option to me, as physically, I was well. And as I wasn't going to operate on patients anyway, why delay? I started as a consultant in my new post on the date indicated on my contract.

Interestingly, without me being informed, my nameplate was removed from the wards where the names of the other consultant surgeons were shown. This was, so I was told later, to avoid any further publicity and to avoid any unnecessary distress to patients who might have seen me on television. No consideration was given by management to any distress that I would feel as a result of this action. I once again had that feeling of being merely a foreigner and a stranger with no one to care for me in this world.

I worked in outpatient clinics and performed gastroscopy and colonoscopy examinations, as these did not risk transferring infection. In addition to taking over the teaching and training rotas for medical students, I became more and more involved in the administration of the unit. A locum consultant was attached to my team so that he could perform some simple surgical operations that I was no longer allowed to do. I could advise him as required but could not go into the operating theatre myself. In addition, I found that patients seen by me at my outpatient clinics who needed major surgery had to be passed on to other consultant surgical colleagues for further management.

I was not at all happy in this new situation. Unfortunately, the hepatitis did not clear up as quickly as I'd hoped it would. This meant, in effect, that, in my surgical practise, when I diagnosed a cancer in a patient in my outpatient clinic, I had to speak to one of my consultant colleagues to arrange surgical treatment. This often proved difficult, as the other surgeons were naturally busy, and for them, taking on other major cases was not easy! I also found it extremely stressful going from consultant to consultant looking for someone to take over the surgical management of my patients. This was not what I had been trained to do. I soon came to the conclusion that I was no longer working as a consultant surgeon, despite the management's arrangement to honour my contract and keep me employed. Something else had to happen!

CHAPTER 14

Change of Direction

After working for about a year in the Victoria Infirmary, things had not improved as far as the hepatitis was concerned. I began to think that my surgical career was coming to a permanent end! Whilst it was very sad to consider giving up surgical practise altogether, after many years of training and experience, I had little choice. In my view, if I could not operate, I could not be a "proper" surgeon. Also, the longer I was out of theatre, the less skilled I would become! I therefore decided that the time had come for me to give up being a surgeon and look for other opportunities to earn a living!

This proved to be immensely difficult. There were very few non-surgical posts advertised that could be considered as suitable alternatives to my present position. Also, to make matters even more difficult, when reasonable posts did become available, they tended to be based in London. After praying and thinking about the matter, I made up my mind that I would take whatever reasonable post came my way, even if it meant working in London.

Having decided to go down this route, I found a post advertised in the *British Medical Journal* that seemed a reasonable possibility. This post was part-time working as an internal surgical adviser to the National Health Service ombudsman. The ombudsman at that time was responsible for investigating and dealing with all kinds of complaints from people against National Health Service staff throughout the whole of the United

Kingdom. The office was in the Millbank Tower in central London. I applied for the post and, after interview, was offered the post. The ombudsman asked if I was considering moving to London. I indicated that I had recently moved to a new house from the East of Scotland to the West of Scotland, and for the moment, I would prefer to travel in from Glasgow to London as required. To my surprise, this was agreed to.

My weekly programme now changed to working part-time for the NHS and part-time for the ombudsman. I worked in the Victoria Infirmary all day on a Monday and Tuesday. At teatime on Tuesday, I left Glasgow, catching a flight to London. I would stay overnight in a hotel and then work for the ombudsman on Wednesday and Thursday before flying back to Glasgow on Thursday night. I then worked at the Victoria Infirmary on the Friday. This became my usual weekly programme.

In addition, after negotiations with the ombudsman, I agreed to a salary, equivalent to 40 per cent of my NHS salary, being paid directly to the NHS for my work for the ombudsman. There was no financial gain for me for doing this work. I did, however, feel a little better in myself, as I had found it extremely uncomfortable receiving a high salary as a consultant surgeon but not performing surgery!

This new arrangement pleased the management greatly. They were delighted to have my input in teaching and training of medical students in a teaching hospital, as well as all the other duties I performed. In addition, they now had a locum surgeon working for them and were receiving a 40 per cent subsidy of my salary. This had never happened before. They were content to let this situation continue for as long as I wanted.

I managed to do both part-time jobs for about a year without a great deal of difficulty. I did often wonder, however, why all this had happened to me. I thought that, with all the surgical experience and skills I had acquired over the years, I was at a level at which I could make the greatest contribution to NHS patients. If this was correct, why had God allowed me to get to this very high level in surgery only to give it up? There did not appear to be any good answer to this ongoing question.

One day, I was on my way back from London. I was standing with many others in an underground train going to Heathrow Airport. As usual, all seats were occupied. Once again, in my mind, I asked God the question: *Why have you let this happen to me?*

I did not receive a direct answer. Instead, I received a question from God in answer to my question! God's question to me was this: "Do you trust me or not?" The answer to that question was a definite yes from me. This finally ended my search for answers, and I simply awaited events knowing that God was still in control.

One night on my arrival home from London, my wife began to share with me some of her ongoing concerns. I thought I was coping quite well with my weekly travel to London. She felt that I was looking more and more tired, and she took the view that I could not go on at the pace I was working at for much longer.

But what else could I do? I had become a chronic carrier of hepatitis B, and there did not appear to be any definitive treatment available. So, all I could do was carry on as I was doing until something else became available. But what would that be?

Amazingly, in God's providence, just then, another interesting post became available. This was a post based in Glasgow. It was advertised by a doctors' trade union known as the Medical and Dental Defence Union of Scotland (MDDUS).

The MDDUS was looking for a qualified and experienced general medical practitioner to work, on a full-time basis, in their central office in Glasgow. The person appointed would help doctor members going through all kinds of personal and professional difficulties throughout the United Kingdom.

Whilst this post seemed a reasonable way forward, there were a few obvious difficulties. Firstly, the MDDUS was looking for a general practitioner, and I had no experience in general practise. Also, there would be no turning back, as this was a full-time permanent appointment! I would have to resign from my NHS consultant post, and there would no going back.

I was not at all convinced that this was the right job for me. However, my wife was keen for me to apply. After all, she argued, this was the first and only reasonable post that had been advertised based in Glasgow where we now lived. I should, at least, make some initial enquiries. I, with her pushing me, agreed to write to the chief executive of the MDDUS to see what would happen. I thought that doing so would at least keep my wife happy. I fully expected to be told there was no point in my applying, as the post was for an experienced "general practitioner", which was clearly not me.

To my surprise, the MDDUS chief executive phoned my secretary and left a message, asking me to come and see him in his office. When we met up, he informed me that there had been a sudden and unexpected change in MDDUS's circumstances. There were several general practitioners as full-time advisers in the union but only one adviser who had been a consultant in the NHS. That consultant had just resigned his post and was returning to clinical practise. MDDUS had a very large of number of doctors applying for their advertised post. And it was decided that there was no need to re-advertise. I would be welcome to apply!

This came as a real surprise. I felt that something was happening here that was out of my control but that I should put in an application and await events. After all, it was now two years since the hepatitis episode had begun, and there appeared to be no significant change in my condition.

A few days later, I received a telephone call from the chief executive again, advising me that I was on the short list and that the MDDUS interviewing panel had asked all candidates coming for interview to prepare a PowerPoint presentation. This was to be five minutes long, and the subject was to be anything relating to the medico-legal aspect of medical practise.

As soon as the call with the chief executive had ended, I immediately had five thoughts in my mind concerning the required PowerPoint presentation. All five began with the letter C. These were "competence"; "compassion"; "confidentiality"; "consent"; and, of course, "cover" from a medical defence organisation.

Just then, our daughter happened to phone me for a chat. I explained to her what was happening and asked her what she thought of my forthcoming five-point presentation. She agreed that it sounded very reasonable. So, I went ahead and prepared a PowerPoint presentation with these five 'C' points for the interview.

The interview went reasonably well. All the members of the MDDUS board, consisting of about ten people, constituted the appointment committee. All of them asked me a question! I tried to be as honest as I could, and told them that, had it not been for my hepatitis, I would not be here. Working as a medico-legal adviser was not my first choice. But given the circumstances I was in, this seemed a very reasonable alternative. I would be able to use much of my experience in clinical medicine at all levels, as well as my management experience at senior level, to assist members. It was interesting for me to note that, whilst every member of the board asked me a question, the chief executive decided not to do so and made no comment.

I heard nothing that day from the MDDUS after the interview, which took place on a Friday morning. I therefore assumed that I had been unsuccessful in obtaining a post. When I went back to work on the Monday, I was approached by one of the consultants at the hospital. He was an accident and emergency consultant who also served on the board of the MDDUS. He came looking for me with a view to informing me that I had been successful in obtaining a post with the MDDUS. The chief executive had tried to contact me all weekend but, despite several phone calls, had not been successful in reaching me. It turned out that this was due to a change in our telephone number, which had occurred after the submission of my CV. I had naturally given the current telephone number at the time. I was therefore asked to confirm my acceptance of the offered MDDUS post by my consultant colleague.

On seeing the details of the contract given to me, I noticed that the salary being offered was far too low. It was more in line with that of someone in the early stages of a medical career, rather than that of someone at my senior level. Thus, I had to say that I could not accept the post and gave my reason for taking that position.

The thing that happened next changed my mind completely about accepting the position being offered to me. To my complete surprise, I had a visitor from the MDDUS. It was none other than the chairman of the MDDUS board himself. He had come to see me at the Victoria Infirmary in order to persuade me to come and work for MDDUS. He explained what MDDUS's position was on the available salaries and offered to raise the initial offer.

I said immediately that I would now accept the post, no matter what salary they were able to offer me! My reasoning was that, whilst financial consideration was, of course, important, other matters should also be considered. Given that the chairman of the MDDUS had paid me such a compliment in that he was prepared to come to my hospital to speak to me personally, that was enough for me. It was obvious that the MDDUS were serious about having me work for the organisation, and whatever it could pay was enough. I would accept the post.

When I went to see the chief executive, after having accepted the post, he told me why I'd obtained this post against some very serious competition. In addition to my extensive clinical and managerial experience, I was the only person on the huge list of interviewees who had worked for the ombudsman! No one else had that experience. Also, he said, my PowerPoint presentation had gone down extremely well. He then told me he was the most experienced medico-legal adviser in the United Kingdom, and after his considerable experience in that field, he'd developed a presentation, which he used often. He knew I hadn't seen his presentation and had been overcome to see me presenting mine. He called his presentation "The Seven C's," and my "five C's" were the first of his seven! I said jokingly, "I was only given five minutes for the presentation!"

On hearing this from the chief executive, I knew right away this was what God had in mind for me. I was to spend the rest of my working life as a MDDUS medico-legal adviser helping other doctors, rather than looking after patients! It was not something I had ever thought about doing, but God knows best!

When I handed in my resignation to the NHS, to my surprise, I had a visit from one of the senior human resources managers. He had come to say how sorry he was that I was leaving. He took the view that, given the situation as it now stood, things could not be much better for the Victoria Hospital. Not only did the hospital have the benefit of my expertise in surgical outpatient clinics, endoscopy clinics, and surgical management issues, I was also teaching and training medical students so well that all my consultant colleagues said it had never been done so well before. In addition, they also had 40 per cent of my salary given back to them. They were very sorry to lose me. Was I sure I should be resigning my post, as I was welcome to continue till retirement?! Whilst this was a great compliment, I said that it was clear to me that my time to leave surgery had come, and I needed to move on.

On commencement of my post with MDDUS, in addition to in-house training, I had to go back to Glasgow University for three years, as a part-time student. This was to study for a master of philosophy degree in medico-legal Issues. This was an interesting experience. I was older than most of my university lecturers. I passed the MPHIL on the first attempt and went back to Glasgow University once again for a graduation ceremony. Many of the parents who had come to see their children graduate, thought that I was one of the professors, not one of the students!

On starting as senior medico-legal adviser for the MDDUS, I soon discovered there were serious issues relating to the payment of the advisers. They were all being paid in random fashion. I suppose part of the reason for this issue being raised was the result of the salary I was going to be paid. Some may have thought I was being paid a high salary even though I had just begun as a medical adviser, whilst they had been working for MDDUS for years. Whilst agreeing that they had a reasonable point, I felt there should be a recognised salary scale agreed on, with management considering all the previous experience and expertise brought to MDDUS by all the medical and dental staff. As a new chief executive had just been appointed, now was the time to have such a discussion.

To my surprise, they all indicated they did not have much experience in negotiating with management about salary scales and wondered if I could do the necessary negotiation on all their behalves. I indicated that I would be honoured to do so and would like to have another representative from the medical advisers' side, as well as an adviser from the dental advisers to join me. They would not have to say anything at the meeting with management, but it would be in our best interests for them to be present.

The negotiation with the new chief executive and board members went very well. I indicated that, if the MDDUS wanted experienced doctors to leave the NHS to work for them, they would have to offer a salary scale that was at least equivalent to what they were accustomed to receiving or they would not attract the right people. This not only led to an agreed good salary scale for the advisers, partly based on my consultant surgeon salary with the NHS, but it also included the equivalent of 20 per cent of our salary, as a non-contributory sum, into a pension pot for us all. This agreement delighted my colleagues, particularly as the BMA, our professional trade union, also agreed that this was an excellent outcome.

I worked for the MDDUS for eleven years and had some wonderful experiences helping my fellow doctors in all kinds of difficulty. It was suggested I should call myself "Dr Mohammed", rather than "Mr Mohammed". I was, of course, accustomed to being addressed as "Mr Mohammed", which was the usual case for surgeons. "Dr Mohammed", however, so it was thought, would avoid me being mistaken for a lawyer. I was content to accept this advice. Furthermore, this was reasonable, as I was no longer working as a surgeon anyway.

It was amazing how often, when I was speaking to doctors over the phone, the doctors would stop speaking and ask if I was Mr Mohammed the surgeon! On hearing my positive response, they often said, "I wondered if that was the case." I suppose there were not too many surgeons called Mr Mohammed around at the time who spoke over the phone with a Scottish accent!

On one occasion, I was advising a general practitioner over the telephone who was having a difficult time with his colleagues—so much so there was a real possibility the practise would have to be closed. They just could not get on well together. As I was making some suggestions as to what he should do to resolve matters, he suddenly interrupted me in our conversation and asked me if he could ask me a personal question. I was not sure where he was coming from but said, yes, he could.

At that, he simply asked me, "Are you a man of faith by any chance?"

I explained that I was, and despite my name, I followed the Lord Jesus Christ.

He told me he was not surprised. I was apparently using terms such as "turn the other cheek" and other such biblical phrases. He then told me there was no need for me to help him any further. He knew exactly what he had to do to bring about a permanent resolution to his practise problems. So, it turned out to be the case that a major problem was averted!

On another occasion, I was helping the legal team in the case of a general practitioner reported to the General Medical Council for alcohol abuse. She was very upset and stressed out—so much so that our lawyer and barrister came to me saying that she was not helping herself and was literally uncontrollable. They asked me to speak to her in private and get her to calm down and be honest with the GMC; otherwise, she would be struck off. They just could not reach her and wondered if I could try. It was amazing to see how often doctors would not trust even their own lawyers!

On speaking to her privately, I discovered several things. She was certainly drinking heavily because she and her husband had split up. She was about to lose her house, as she could not pay the mortgage. She was also worried about time needed to look after her son. There appeared to be no way out. If she were to be struck off by the GMC, as seemed very likely, that would be the straw that broke the proverbial Camel's back! If that were to happen, her life would be utterly ruined.

On further discussion with her about her life in general, I discovered that she was from a Roman Catholic background. I was thus able to speak to her about Jesus and how he could help her when no one else could. She needed to have faith in Him and to pray for help. She also needed to be honest with the GMC about her weakness and why she was in that position. She appeared to take in my advice quite well. On her request, I said a little prayer, and she was then called in to face the GMC panel.

She sat down in front of the GMC and took the oath to tell the truth. She broke down in tears and told the GMC her position and the reason for it. She was honest and truthful in what she said. She promised to seek further advice from alcoholic anonymous to stop drinking.

To everyone's surprise, the GMC panel became very supportive, and instead of stopping her continuing in the practise of medicine, as everyone had expected would be the outcome, they allowed her to continue under GMC condition and supervision. She thus could continue working and keep her home and was also able to look after her son. What an outcome!

Over the next few months, she made a good recovery and stopped drinking alcohol. She also managed to switch from general practise to working in a hospital. Sometime later, I was pleased to receive a letter from her thanking me for my support. She also wrote that I would never know how much what I'd said before the GMC panel hearing had meant to her!

Whilst many people have asked me if I missed doing surgery, I have had to reply quite honestly, "Not really!" In fact, some years later, the professor of infectious diseases who was looking after me started me on a new medication. This reduced my hepatitis B to virtually undetectable levels. He asked me when I was going to go back to surgery. He was disappointed to hear my response that I would not be going back into surgery. I had been out of surgery for too long a period and trying to go back was not practical. After all, I had come into medical practise and surgery to help people. I was still doing that through the MDDUS. This was what the Lord had for me. I was still helping people, though not through surgery anymore.

However, after working for the MDDUS for eleven years, I decided it was time to retire. I handed in my resignation, giving six months' notice as required. I thought this would be the end of my working life.

Just then, I had a visit from the chief executive. We had previously discussed an idea of mine to have a "telephone team" available for members to get instant advice for straightforward cases, as this would open up time for the medical advisers to spend on more complex issues. He suggested that, instead of retiring, I could work on a part-time basis from home as the leader of a telephone team. He took the view that it might be good for me to step down a little before retiring completely. In addition, it would be very helpful for him, as he did not have anyone else available who could help in this way. I agreed to this suggestion and ended up working three days a week from home for the next two years, before retiring completely at the age of sixty-five.

To be honest, why, at the very height of my career, I had to give up surgery, still remains bit of a mystery. But, having said that, the answer I received from God to this question remains the answer. Namely, "Do I trust God or not?"

If I trust Him, then I must accept that, as God, He is in control and plans all things after the council of his own will. He is also planning for eternity, not just for time. When eternity dawns, and I know just as I am known, then the full answer will be revealed. I am certain that, on hearing His full answer, I will fall on my knees and praise God for everything He has done and will marvel at his wisdom! Till then, we walk by faith and not by sight.

CHAPTER 15

Family Matters

There is little doubt that growing up as a child in Glasgow was difficult and often lonely for me. I did have three brothers, of course, but we did not seem to be very close to one another. In addition, I had no real friends. When I became a Christian, in some way, life became even worse! I remember when I first started to attend a church regularly; the other young people would often meet for fun and fellowship on a Saturday night in various church members' homes. I was never invited.

I also recall once speaking at a meeting where I was asked to tell something of my testimony. This meant basically telling people something of what had happened to me at Golspie High School and why I had become a follower of Jesus Christ. I, of course, encouraged others to follow Jesus if they were not already followers.

After the meeting came to an end, an elderly lady came over to speak to me. She told me that she had been a missionary somewhere in Asia for several years and knew about the Muslim culture well. She wanted to tell me that there would be one difficulty for me, as I was now a Christian. That was, to put it simply, I would never be able to get a wife!

Asian marriages were arranged in a particular way. To get married, I would have to ask my father to approach the father of any suitable girl and seek consent from him for me to marry his daughter. She said that I would never get that permission, so I would remain single all my life! I found these comments "interesting"—not that I was thinking of getting married to anyone at that time. However, she was partly right, in that my father did not ever approach me concerning any possible marriage plan for me, though he did arrange the Muslim marriages of my three brothers.

As a form of service to the Lord and as a means of fellowship with Christians, I attended the 428 Club every week. One of the consequences of attending the 428 Club was that I did come across other Christians who were also keen to take the message of Jesus to others. As I had some interest in playing the guitar, not that I was all that good at it, I decided to set up a small musical group to sing hymns and preach at church services as the opportunity arose. In those days, there were many small churches that had Saturday night tea meetings and, as many had no pastors, they were keen to have visiting musical bands and lay preachers to lead these services. It was often said jokingly that, in those days, there were more church meetings than pubs in Glasgow!

One young lady who had a wonderful singing voice was keen to join our group. So, together with another two guitar players, we set up a band to sing hymns and present the gospel message at these meetings. This young lady was a Christian and attended the 428 Club every week. In fact, she had been involved in the 428 Club from when it first started years earlier.

The group went around various churches as invited, singing and preaching the gospel. I was very impressed by our leading lady's singing voice. She knew all the Christian songs and could harmonise very well. Her name was Janet. We developed a close platonic friendship for a couple of years, which then led to a more romantic relationship.

She told me later, when we started to go out together, that she remembered seeing me when I first started to come to the 428 Club. She said that, one night, I was asked to say the opening prayer. She had her eyes shut and was listening. She heard my prayer and thought to herself, what a wonderful voice that person has and what a wonderful prayer. She had not heard that voice before and wondered who the person was. So, she rather naughtily opened her eyes to see who it was that was praying. It was then she saw that it was me.

When we started to go out together on romantic dates, my fellow band members became a little concerned as to how things would progress between us. They were worried about what people would say if we became more serious in our relationship, given our different ethnicities. Also, looking ahead, if we were to get married and had children, what would happen to them? To whom would they belong? These were some serious questions that needed to be addressed.

What should we do? Should we just bring our relationship to an end? Certainly, some people would not approve of our relationship, even though we were sensible adults and perfectly able to make our own decisions? Does one simply follow the rules and regulations that appear to exist in the society you happen to belong to?

More importantly for me, however, there did not appear to be any prohibition on our being together in the scriptures. It seemed to me that I was free to marry any woman who was single and a Christian and, of course, prepared to marry me.

Despite all the questions raised, for which there were no easy answers, we were content to become engaged to be married. The wedding would take place in a year's time, when I would be qualifying as a doctor. I had no other option anyway. I would, hopefully, be able to acquire married accommodation for the first year in the hospitals in which I would be working. This would allow me to save up and have some capital for the first time in my life. This then would let me get a mortgage to buy a house of some sort after that year was up. Janet worked as a full-time secretary, and her salary would be enough to take care of our daily needs.

Things worked out just as planned. We were married on the July 17, 1974, in the Glasgow University Chapel. It was possible to be married there if one person getting married was a graduate of the university. As this was a very special occasion for us, and the small church building in Bridgeton where we worshiped was not very suitable for a wedding in any case, this seemed to be the best solution. Our pastor was surprisingly keen for us to marry in Glasgow University Chapel. He indicated that he was looking forward to taking part in the ceremony very much. He had never officiated a wedding in such a place before and was not likely to have another chance of doing so again.

There was not a great deal of interest in my family concerning my forthcoming wedding. However, on the day of the ceremony itself, to my surprise, Mum came to the chapel, accompanied by one of my younger brothers. They did not stay for the whole day, but it was wonderful to have them present for the Christian wedding ceremony.

Three ministers took part in our marriage ceremony. These were the pastor of the church in Bridgeton that we had both joined, a minister friend, and a minister of Indian origin who had been appointed by the Church of Scotland to minister to the Asian community in Glasgow.

All the members of the church were there as our guests and came to support us and to rejoice with us on our special day. The highlight of the night of celebration was Janet singing a solo at the reception. She sang a song called "My Task" (written by Maude Louise Ray), which began with the words, "To love someone more dearly every day." She was accompanied on the piano by my close friend from secondary school. It turned out to be a great day never to be forgotten! For once in my life, I felt as though I somehow belonged.

My best man at our wedding was a young man I got to know well through the seaside mission. We became very close friends. He was studying for the ministry. Sadly, as always seems to happen, certainly to me, this time of joy was soon followed by a time of great sadness. My best man soon developed kidney failure, and despite all possible treatment, his condition deteriorated.

Together, another mutual Christian friend (who later became a minister) and I anointed him with oil and prayed for his healing as indicated in the Bible. Sad to say, his condition continued to deteriorate, and sometime later, he passed away from this life. Rest in peace, dear friend!

For our honeymoon, Janet and I went to a small hotel just outside Athens. The cost of this was paid for by Janet's parents. It was a wonderful time, with the summer sun glowing and an almost empty seashore to walk along every day. We managed to visit Athens itself and see the magnificent buildings, including the Parthenon, that all tourists are interested in.

I was particularly taken by a small plaque, which did not seem to be of great interest to anyone else. This plaque was on "Mars Hill", where it was stated that Paul the Apostle had spoken to the Athenians about Jesus. I found it fascinating to see the confirmation of biblical history in such a way. I was so overcome to see the plaque that I spent a great deal of time just standing looking at it. I did not realise that I was holding up everyone else sitting in the bus, which was ready to take us back to our hotel. Luckily, Janet was wise enough to shout at me and tell me that it was time to go.

In the latter part of our holiday, something quite unexpected happened. Suddenly, all the men of the village left to go to the capital, leaving only the women. The television programmes stopped, and only military music was broadcast. Clearly, Greece was at war. It was impossible to know what was going on, especially as we did not speak the local language. We could listen to the BBC World News, which interestingly seemed to be the most trustworthy news channel of all. Even the local Greek people crowded round to hear the BBC news broadcast. The news seemed to come across as though Turkey had invaded Greece. We were than informed that all the young men had to report to their allocated military centres for the defence of their country, or they would be shot. Hence, all the men left immediately, commandeering any vehicle they could.

Later, it became clear that Turkey had, in fact, invaded the island called Cyprus, which belonged to Greece, and not mainland Greece itself. We seemed to be safe enough but were concerned that there could be difficulty getting out of Greece, as it was unclear when the airports would be opened. Also, as there were no men available in the hotel, this meant there were no waiters. The tourists were not too happy, as this meant the service they were receiving was not up to expected standards. Janet and I ended up by helping to clear the tables, much to the surprise of the female staff. We felt that this was the least we could do to help a country at war!

It was wonderful that, in the providence of God, we could fly back to Scotland safely and on time to start my hospital job as planned. We could not, however, help but notice the presence of numerous tanks in the streets of Athens as we made our way to the airport. It wasn't a pleasant experience for us, especially on our honeymoon.

We didn't have a great deal of contact with our respective families until sometime later when our son Mark was born. That changed things considerably. Janet's mum and dad, who were not Christians, were delighted to see their first grandson. Thereafter, they became just normal loving grandparents, which resulted in deepening of relationships. Similarly, my eldest brother and his family became interested in seeing

Mark. This led to some re-engagement with that part of the family as well. Mum, on seeing Mark for the first time, asked me if I was going to have him circumcised. This is, of course, a recognised Islamic custom. She was disappointed to hear my negative response. I don't think she saw Mark again.

Whilst the birth of our son was a wonderful occasion, we did have to go through a previous major difficulty. When Janet became pregnant for the first time, we were both delighted. It seemed that life could not get any better.

Then tragedy struck! It became clear, quite early in the pregnancy, that there was a serious problem. A major genetic malformation was diagnosed, and not unexpectedly, Janet lost the baby. I was utterly devastated.

I had just begun to feel that I was no longer just a foreigner and all alone in this life after all. No. I was going to be a father! I would have, and be part of, a "proper" family. When we lost the baby, I found it very difficult to cope with the loss. I was angry with God. I could not understand why God would let this happen to me—especially given what I had been through with my own family. He was eternal and all powerful. He could have easily prevented this from happening. Why didn't He? What was the purpose of letting this happen, especially to someone like me? I did not receive an answer from the Lord concerning this matter. I just had to trust and wait. It was not an easy time!

However, about a year later, when our son, Mark, was born and I got to hold him in my arms for the very first time, all my questions and worries disappeared forever. It was as though the Lord was saying to me, "This is my answer. What do you think now?" On looking at my newborn son's face, I had no more questions to ask. I could not help but praise and thank God for His love, mercy, and grace.

Being a father and having a son was more than enough for me! I just could not love him more. My wife, Janet, however, was not satisfied. She was the only child in her family and had decided a long time ago that she would not have only one child herself; she wanted another. She had her way as usual, and I was so glad that she did! For our daughter, Sylvia, was born some twenty-one months later.

It was utterly amazing to see her being born by a straightforward natural birth. I was able to be present throughout the whole of the birth process, supporting my wife when Sylvia was born. I had, of course, seen mothers giving birth on several occasions as a medical student, but it was so different when it was your own wife giving birth to your own daughter. It was a wonderful and unforgettable occasion. Hearing my daughter starting to cry for the first time just after her birth brought tears to my eyes too.

I then discovered something incredible about love that I had not fully grasped before. I discovered that, whilst I loved my son Mark so much that I just could not love him more, when Sylvia came along, I did not need to half my love for him to love Sylvia. Rather, my love just grew to include her as well, and I found myself loving them both equally. They were the best gifts that God had ever given me. No one can beat God at giving.

Among some of the wonderful memories I have of them growing up was the occasion when, on one evening, I gave them both a bath. They were both young enough to have a bath together. After the bath, we needed to decide whose bedroom we would go into to dry them both. As each of them had a room of their own in our house, it was a decision that needed to be made.

Whilst we were talking about whose room to use, I said to them both, "Did you know that both of you have a room in God's house in heaven as well?"

They did not know that. Mark asked, "Do I really have a room in God's house in heaven?"

"Yes, you do," I said. "But there's one problem."

"What's the problem?" he asked.

"Well," I said, "you have a room. But it does not have your name on the door."

"Oh," he said. "That's not good. How do I get my name on my room in heaven?"

I said that the only way I knew to make sure his name was on his door in heaven was to ask Jesus to be his friend and ask Jesus to put his name on his door. "That way, when you die and go to heaven, your room will be there waiting for you," I explained.

Mark at once replied, "I know what you mean, Dad. It's like phoning a restaurant to book a table when you are going to go there next week."

125

Yes, I agreed. That was right. I then asked if he would like to ask Jesus to put his name on his door in heaven.

He replied, "Yes, I would like to ask Jesus to do that right now."

So we said a prayer, and Mark decided to write his name on a form we had available related to becoming a Christian. What a wonderful moment.

At this point, Sylvia, who had been silent but was obviously listening to what was going on, spoke up and said, "It would not be for me. I would not be allowed, as I am too young."

Holding back the tears in my eyes, I reassured her that she was not too young, even at five years of age. If she wanted Jesus to put her name on her door, that would be allowed, and Jesus would do it right away.

Mark, of course, as the big brother, spoke up and encouraged her to do what he was doing and even offered to help her write her name on the form he was using.

Next, the question arose about how good the room would be. I said that, whilst their rooms were now both booked, both rooms were just empty. The rooms had no toys, pictures, mirrors, furniture, or carpets in them. However, they could start decorating their heavenly room by how they lived their lives here. If they were kind to others and did good deeds, God would notice that, even if no one else did, and God would arrange for, say, a painting to be put up on a wall in their room. If they did other good things, such as tell their friends about Jesus, that would be rewarded as well. In this way, they could gradually decorate their rooms in heaven. When, in the future, they were ready to go to their heavenly home, only then would they see how wonderful the decorations in their room were. That was a wonderful day, one I will never forget!

Both our children attended church regularly with us all their young lives. I remember one evening when we attended church in Dunfermline, where I had just obtained a consultant post, for the evening service. It was a busy Sunday evening, with hundreds of people making their way to a football match in the town. When we got to the church that evening, there were very few people attending the evening service. This had not been the case in our previous church.

Mark, who would have been ten at the time, asked in a loud whisper that probably everyone could hear, "Where are the people, Dad?"

It was a bit embarrassing, but it was a good question.

Both of our children continued to attend church regularly with us in Dunfermline for many years and then continued to do so in Aberdeen where both went to university to study law.

Whilst the children were growing up in Dunfermline, things were not altogether easy for them. Being of mixed race, they sadly had their own issues to face, particularly at the local secondary school. We were not aware of the difficulties they were facing. They, however, faced these problems and difficulties courageously and dealt with them without too much assistance from parents. In retrospect, I wonder if things might have been easier for them had I chosen to send them to a private school rather than the local school. I was never keen to send my children to a fee-paying school, as I did not then think that using wealth to "buy privilege" was fair. I suppose we will never know.

Whilst some Christian friends, in the early days, were concerned that our marriage may not last very long, I am sure they would be glad to know that Janet and I celebrated our fortieth (ruby) wedding anniversary, in 2014. This was the same year that our daughter Sylvia married her fiancé, Ronan!

One of my greatest difficulties as far as our family history is concerned was facing the sad news of the break-up of our son's marriage. Mark's relationship with his future wife commenced when they were both students at Aberdeen University. From our meeting with my son's future wife, it seemed clear that she had a strong personality, whilst Mark tended to be very much a "fence sitter". They both, however, followed the Christian faith and went to church regularly. We found out, as time went on, that Mark was persuaded to leave the local Baptist church they both attended in order to worship at a Church of Scotland instead. This church was led by an excellent minister, but it did mean that Mark had much less contact with his long-standing friends.

Mark was studying law whilst his future wife studied religious education. After qualifying with their respective degrees, they became engaged to be married, and both moved to live in Edinburgh. When the marriage ceremony drew near, she made it clear that she wanted nobody from either family to be present and considered marriage to be a matter only for her and Mark. Whilst it seemed clear to us that Mark would not in any way mind the presence of the family, he nevertheless did not object. This caused both Janet and I great heartache, as we had expected their marriage to include all family members. As Mark's fiancée could not be persuaded and Mark did as she wanted, they finally went to the island of Barbados by themselves and went through a marriage ceremony there.

Mark phoned from Barbados after the ceremony to tell me that all had gone very well. He also mentioned that, quite unexpectedly, they had met a couple on the aeroplane who was also going to Barbados. They'd become quite friendly with them—so much so that the two were asked to be witnesses at their wedding. The couple, he said, lived down the road from us. This news made not being there at the wedding even more difficult for Janet and me.

After about three years of married life, Mark concluded that he and his wife could no longer go on living together. Even though almost half of all marriages in the United Kingdom break up, we did not expect this to happen to our son. I suppose no one expects something like this to happen in his or her family. Nevertheless, it was very sad to hear the news that our son's marriage had come to a definite end.

Mark moved out of the marital home thus indicating, from his perspective, that there was no chance of reconciliation, even though, as we soon discovered, his wife was expecting the birth of our first wonderful grandson. Whilst Mark chose to be present at the birth of his son, this did not make any great difference as far as their marriage was concerned. They still went their separate ways.

We found out later that, whilst Mark had shared his concerns about the marriage break-up with his sister, Sylvia, he did not tell us about the difficulties he was facing. I suppose this was his way of trying to protect his parents, as he would know how painful this would be for both mum and dad. Sad as it was to see this happen, we were delighted that at least something great and wonderful had come from the marriage, namely our first grandson, Ethan Ryan.

We lived in Glasgow for about nine years, having moved there from Dunfermline when I was appointed consultant surgeon to work at the Victoria Infirmary. We made it clear to everyone that we would like to have a loving relationship with Ethan and would do all we could to bring that about. To fulfil that promise, Janet would take the train every week to Edinburgh to bring Ethan home for an overnight stay with us in Glasgow. This would allow us to get to know him and would also give his mother some free time, as it was not easy for her being a secondary school teacher and a single mum as she now was!

Ethan loved the train journey and was always very ready to talk, even at three years of age, much to the entertainment of other passengers. When the train from Newton Mearns came into Central Station in Glasgow, an announcement over the loudspeaker would always say, "Welcome. The train is now approaching Glasgow Central Station."

On hearing this announcement, Ethan would always say in a loud voice to anyone listening, "I don't come from Glasgow. I come from Edinburgh"—much to everyone's amusement.

When it became obvious that it would be much easier, especially for Janet, to help look after Ethan if we were nearer to him, we decided to move to Edinburgh. This allowed us to be more easily available for grandparenting duties! In addition, by this time, our son Mark was thinking of becoming an advocate and wasn't likely to move out of Edinburgh either. We told both Mark and his wife that, no matter what decisions they made about their marriage and life, we would continue to love them both and that Ethan would always be our beloved grandson. He would receive our love and support no matter what happened. Our moving to Edinburgh was one practical example of the truth of that statement.

As it so happened, I was, by this time, working as a senior medical adviser for the Medical and Dental Defence Union of Scotland and covering the whole of the United Kingdom. It did not make a great deal of difference whether I lived in Glasgow or Edinburgh. This move, of course, would have been impossible if I had been in surgical practise at the Victoria Infirmary. In the providence of God, by this time, I was no longer in clinical practise. Thus, we could make the move. It was far easier for me to travel into the head office in Glasgow then for Janet to travel to Edinburgh and back with a young boy!

Soon after Mark split up from his wife, he became quite seriously ill. He developed a chronic cough, for which there appeared to be no good and obvious reason. He did not smoke and was very active and fit.

It was not until some lumps began to appear on Mark's neck that appropriate medical intervention took place. He was seen by a consultant surgeon friend of mine, who did a biopsy of one of the lumps. The diagnosis turned out to be advanced Hodgkin's lymphoma, a form of cancer. This meant that he had to undergo months of chemotherapy to try to cure him of this form of cancer.

I was very proud of him when he told me that the consultant in charge of his chemotherapy advised there was a clinical study under way. It was not known which chemotherapy regimen was best. The study consisted of a randomised allocation of patients to either three chemotherapeutic drugs or four. Mark immediately consented to join the study, on the basis that the information may help others in the future.

He was, at that time, working in the legal department of the City of Edinburgh Council. He was told that, while he was having chemotherapy, he could simply take off as much time as he needed, even if it meant he would be off for six months. He refused to do so. Instead, he worked as much as he could during the entire time of his chemotherapy. He would literally be vomiting for a couple of days after the chemotherapy. As soon as he was able, he would make his way to the office and work for the rest of the week. This he continued to do for all the months he received chemotherapy.

I often wondered if the stress of the failure of his marriage was at least partly responsible for him developing this form of cancer. I suppose we will never know. But I was so grateful to the staff of the NHS for the care offered to my son and to God for answering my prayers on his behalf.

I simply asked God, "Is it not the case, that my son should be attending my funeral, rather than me attending his?"

The Lord graciously answered my prayer by ensuring that the chemotherapy was successful, and Mark was clear of the cancer with a negative CT scan some five years after his treatment.

A year or so after the break-up of his marriage, Mark formed a relationship with a lady lawyer he knew in Edinburgh. They soon moved in together into a flat as life partners. Soon they had a child together, and we were blessed to have a granddaughter who was named Catherine Louise. Once again, we made sure that everyone knew, no matter the circumstances, we would love our granddaughter as much as possible. There would be no difference in our love and support for our grandchildren. We encouraged Mark to keep in touch with his son Ethan, despite the inevitable divorce that followed. This he continues to do. We see both our grandchildren every week and have the joy of looking after them overnight. I regard it as a great privilege to be a granddad!

What the future holds for Mark, only God knows. But God also knows from my constant prayers on his behalf what I would like to see happen! I have kept what I would like to see happen in Mark's life to myself, and I await events in faith.

The next family issue that arose concerned our daughter. Sylvia had been working as a lawyer for the Moray Council for a few years and seemed quite content. It came as a great surprise and shock when she informed us that she wanted to give up her post as a lawyer in Elgin to study music in London. Doing so would be a very different experience for her.

When she was younger and did not have a definitive choice in terms of what she wanted as a career when she was leaving secondary school, we agreed that she should go to Aberdeen University and study law there, with her brother to keep an eye on her. After all, she had enough exam passes to study law, and having a law degree would be useful even if she decided not to work as a lawyer.

As things worked out after qualification, she managed to get a traineeship in Aberdeen right away. Thereafter, she was headhunted for a post as a lawyer in Elgin. After working there for a few years, she was not fully satisfied with life. We had agreed previously that, though she was to study law, if she decided to do something else subsequently, we would support her. Now we had to keep the promise we had made earlier.

Moving to London to study music was somewhat different from being a lawyer! Certainly, she always had enjoyed singing and playing the piano. After all, her mother was a very good singer, and music played a big part in her life. Nevertheless, this was unexpected. Also, being a well-paid and self-sufficient lawyer was considerably different to being a full-time student once more and, of course, back on the family budget!

She did some time at Vocal-Tech Music School in London learning how to sing professionally, using her voice as the main instrument. She enjoyed this so much that she decided that the study of music was for her. She proceeded then to do a degree course with the Tech-Music School and, after three years, passed her bachelor of music examination (BMus) at honours level. Her voice was her main instrument, though she did play and teach beginners how to play the piano. Her main ambition was to become a professional backing vocalist and songwriter.

Although moving from law to music was quite a change for her, it was not as great a change as that which was still to come. She met and became engaged to be married to Ronan, a gifted musician who was a university lecturer in music and a professional guitarist. He was born in Ireland but, like Sylvia, had left his home to go to London to study music. They thus had much in common.

The wedding day soon came around. It turned out to be a wonderful occasion held in a place called Crieff Hydro Hotel. Sylvia and Mark had been accustomed to going to the Hydro for many years, as the Christian Medical Fellowship, of which I was a member, held its annual conference there. We attended as a family every year. So, Sylvia and Ronan decided this would be a good venue for the wedding.

I told my brothers about the wedding, which was to take place in some six months' time, and all three brothers seemed quite keen to attend. I was quite excited about having a family wedding at which many people from my side of the family would be able to come. No one had any obvious difficulties in terms of where and when the wedding was to be held. Furthermore, the wedding ceremony being held in a hotel, rather than a church building seemed to be helpful from my brothers' point of view. The conducting of the wedding ceremony by a very close friend, who was well known to Sylvia and who was a teacher and not a Church minister may have been helpful too.

When the day of the wedding came, it turned out to be on the last day of Ramadan, the holy fasting month for Muslims. Whilst my brothers had been told in advance the date of the wedding, as Ramadan is based on the lunar month, no one knew then that there would be a clash. If that had been known, the wedding could easily have been planned to take place a week later.

This was most unfortunate. Because of this, my eldest brother could not attend the wedding, as he was spending the last ten days of Ramadan entirely in the mosque. However, my other two brothers and their families did attend. One brother came only for the reception, after the wedding ceremony. He was fasting and did not eat or drink anything. My youngest brother and his wife, however, made their way from Birmingham and stayed for the whole day. They could do this, as technically, they would be on a "long journey", and this was a legitimate way to avoid fasting till later.

Some days after the wedding, I got a phone call from my brother's wife in Birmingham to say that she'd enjoyed the whole experience very much. This was the first Christian wedding she had ever attended, and she'd never imagined just how wonderful an occasion it would turn out to be.

As Sylvia thought she would soon be too old to have a baby, she and Ronan decided to have a child right away. As a result of this desire, a year later, Sylvia gave birth to a baby boy. This, sadly, turned out to be a very difficult experience for her and Ronan. After a long and painful labour, she needed an emergency Caesarean section. In addition, because of inadequate nursing care in the NHS maternity ward in London, she had to have herself and her baby transferred to the private wing for further proper treatment and nursing care. However, thanks to the grace of God and good private medical care, all went well subsequently, and we were blessed by having another beautiful grandson later named Art Egan.

We, of course, were happy to travel to London to see our wonderful grandson from time to time. As I was travelling to London for work purposes, this gave me another opportunity to catch up with Sylvia.

However, after living in London for a year or so and experiencing work as a supply teacher, she decided that London was not for her or her son. It was a very expensive place to live, and she thought it was not altogether safe. In addition, she missed having Mum and Dad around. She therefore decided the time was right for her to move out of London and go to live elsewhere. The only other reasonable place would be Edinburgh. The problem was that Ronan was working in London and could not leave London, as he couldn't get any reasonable work in the music industry outside of London.

They decided that Sylvia and their son would move to Edinburgh, and Ronan would travel back and forth to see them. They would decide what to do as things developed. Sylvia was also fortunate enough to acquire employment as a lawyer once again, giving up her desire to be a professional musician. This situation continues for them till the present day. What the future holds is still awaited.

We all forget too easily that life moves on, and we are not as young or as able as we were before. Growing old came to my mind not because I had retired from work but because of Janet's physical condition. She was very fit but began to feel more and more pain and stiffness in her left knee. She decided to seek a medical opinion and was soon seen by a consultant orthopaedic surgeon. He advised that she should have her left knee replaced due to severe arthritis. It so happened that we had decided it was the right time to "downsize" our house, and the date for the operation given was just before we were due to move to our new home. She decided to go ahead with the operation on the date given, rather than postpone it. This proved to be a very difficult and stressful time.

It was good to get a phone call from my consultant surgeon friend from Yorkshire, who reminded me that, whilst he and I had done many surgical operations on numerous occasions in the recent past, it was a different situation altogether when it was your wife going through one. So true! Praise God, Janet made a slow but steady recovery from this ordeal.

Whilst, in no way can we say our life is perfect, nevertheless, I am grateful to God for his grace, mercy, and love shown to me and my family. Obviously, it would have been better if I had a closer relationship with all my extended family. But because of my faith in Christ, this was not possible. In all fairness, the Bible does make it clear that he who loves mother or father more than Jesus can't be his disciple. I am, however, encouraged by the knowledge that Jesus had similar family experiences. John the apostle writes, "For neither did his brethren believe in him" (John 7:5, KJV), though things did change subsequently.

We continue to pray that some wonderful change in relationship with the rest of the family will still happen. Nothing is impossible with God.

CHAPTER 16

Church Experience

Having accepted the invitation to follow Jesus, it soon became obvious that I needed to have fellowship with others who had made the same decision. There was no possibility of going back to a Mosque to worship God, as those present there would not accept me. The fact that I believed Jesus could visit me and invite me to follow him, leaving everything else behind, including the religion of Islam, was totally unacceptable. The only way for someone like me to be accepted by the Islamic community would be to renounce my Christian convictions. I would have to be prepared to accept that God was Allah and Muhammad was his prophet and the only way to paradise was by following the way of Islam. Whilst I never had any difficulty in believing that there could only be one God, and Allah was just an Arabic name for God, I could no longer, in good conscience, follow what was written in the Koran as being the final word of God.

But where would an Asian young man like me find a place for fellowship and worship in Bridgeton? I did not know. I did get literature through the letter box from people who called themselves the Jehovah's Witnesses. I had no idea who they were, but I had read about Jehovah in the Bible and so tried to read what was written in the cards they delivered. The literature put through the letter box seemed to concentrate very much around blood transfusions. Something inside me seemed to indicate that this type of literature was not for me, and so the literature went into the bin.

Sadly, despite having lived in Bridgeton for over eleven years by this time, I had not received any literature from any church or Christian organisation with an invitation to come and worship with them.

After agreeing to meet the man who told me he had lost his Bible at the 428 Club, I began to attend there on a regular basis. It was here that I happened to meet up with my friend who also had been influenced by the same person at the school camp. He also started to attend the 428 Club. He mentioned to me that he was now going for two weeks during the summer holidays to a Church of Scotland Seaside Mission, which was an outreach to young people and others by a group of Christians going and living in towns near the seashore. He wondered if I would like to accompany him to one of these seaside missions to be held in Aberdeen.

As I had never been taken for a family summer holiday before and, as summer holidays were not possible given my family situation at the time, I decided to give the seaside mission idea a try. I did not know much about what would happen and what I would have to do, but it didn't seem to matter. I was going "on holiday" with Christian friends. This was exciting!

Due to the preaching and teaching at the 428 Club, I began to understand a little bit more about what the church was meant to be, and that we should all, as believers, witness to the saving faith in Jesus Christ. Hence, going on seaside mission seemed very reasonable. It would be more than just a holiday.

On the seaside mission in Aberdeen, I met up with about fifteen other young people who formed the team. We stayed in a local Church of Scotland building and slept on the floor. We all had to play our part in terms of cleaning and cooking. There was a fee to be paid for the cost of the holiday, which I could not, in fact, fully afford. However, due to the grace of God, I was not embarrassed. The minister in charge of the seaside mission made it abundantly clear that the amount to be paid was only a guide; we would each be welcome to put into the finance box only as much or as little we could afford. Only God would know how much each person had contributed for the expense of the mission outreach.

As I only had two pound coins, I went to the contribution box and was about to put both coins in when something in my head said, *Put only one coin in and keep the other for further use.* I listened to that voice and only put in one coin.

That evening, it was announced that the whole team needed a rest time and that we would all be going on a bus to a nearby park for a picnic. It was, however, necessary for everyone to contribute one pound to help cover the cost. This was not confidential, as the money would be collected by the treasurer. I just praised God for his kindness to me, as I could openly give a pound coin like everyone else without any embarrassment. I knew then why the voice in my mind had told me to keep one coin in my pocket.

I learnt a lesson that was to be with me for the rest of my life. It was simply this. God does not look at what you give but what you have left after you have given! Hence, Jesus observed the rich giving money openly for all to see and then saw the old lady put a few small coins into the offering box and said that she had given more than them all, as she had given God everything she owned.

Over the two-week seaside mission period, I was fortunate enough to strike up a friendship with a young man who had no faith. I invited him to come along to our evening meetings when members of the seaside mission team would explain the reason for their faith. He began to attend the meetings held by the team regularly, and at the end of the second week, he indicated that he wanted to become a Christian. I took him to meet the minister who was the leader of the team. The minister, after some discussion, decided that the young man was genuine in his request to become a Christian and so prayed with him, and the young man accepted Christ as his saviour.

Whilst everyone in the team was happy to see the young man make this decision, I found it very difficult, even though I was the one who had befriended him and invited him to come to the meetings! I was challenged by this young man's confession of faith. The reason for this was that, whilst I was a follower of Jesus, there remained a particular difficulty for me. This was mainly about who Jesus Christ was.

I had been taught since childhood that Jesus, though a good person and a prophet of God, was only a human being. On the other hand, I had met Jesus in Golspie High School, and I was reading in the Bible that

Jesus was one with God. What was the truth? My Christian friends on the seaside mission seemed to have no difficulty in believing that Jesus was God in the flesh, whilst I struggled with accepting this concept fully. Furthermore, I had been responsible for helping to bring a person to Jesus, yet I had difficulty in my mind and heart believing who Jesus really was! Was that not hypocrisy? I felt I could not go on any longer without sorting out this difficulty in my mind.

So, I went into the prayer room in the church we were staying in. I fell on my knees before God and asked for His help. It seemed to me that I was being hypocritical telling others about Jesus and asking them to trust in Him but could not fully believe in Him myself. I asked God to help me to believe. I needed His help because of my Muslim background and the difficulty it gave me in believing in the nature of God and Jesus.

I am glad to say that I got up from my knees and no longer had a problem in believing who Jesus really was! After all, the simple fact was that God had revealed something of his nature to humankind by becoming human. Who was I say to say that God could not do that? He, being God, had no limitations. He could do anything, even beyond human understanding. Furthermore, who would be good enough to be able to pay the price for the salvation of millions of human beings by one death on the Cross? Surely, only God could pay the needed price. This truth had not been invented by man but, rather, revealed by God in the scriptures.

From then on, during my university student days, I attended the seaside mission every year. These two weeks during summer became my holiday. I worked the rest of the summer, as I had no other choice. I remember my medical student friends mentioning to me the many exotic holidays they went on during the long summer breaks we all had. I was happy just going to Troon for two weeks in the summer to serve the Lord with others on the seaside mission.

This time of service on the seaside mission was a great privilege for me. I remember getting to know one little girl particularly well at the beach games and chorus singing we used to do. In those days, you could carry young girls around six or seven years of age on your shoulders! This little girl wanted me to come to her home and meet her mum. I did do so and found that her dad was a local GP. Her mum told me how much her daughter liked me and was enjoying attending the activities of the seaside mission. Having met me and knowing that I was a medical student seemed to give her some reassurance that I was trustworthy and that all was well for her daughter. When the seaside mission fortnight came to an end, I gave a Bible to the little girl as a present. I did not see her again.

When I was a consultant and developed hepatitis B, resulting in much unwanted media attention, I received, literally, hundreds of cards from all over the country. One card stood out for me. It was from a lady who wrote to say that she remembered me from seaside mission in Troon nearly thirty years earlier and was sorry to see that I had developed hepatitis, and she wished me well. It was so moving and encouraging to read this letter. God had not forgotten me or the service I'd rendered when I was a medical student.

After experiencing the fun and fellowship at seaside mission, my friend from school and I decided that we should start attending church regularly. He had been to Sunday school many years ago, in a small evangelical church called the Bethany Hall in Bridgeton. This was within walking distance from my home, and so we started attending this small church. The church did not have a minister. Rather, a few elders ran the church. It had excellent worship music led by a dentist who played the piano extremely well. Soon my friend and I started attending the church choir, which met regularly.

I remember well the one occasion when I went with the men's choir to Northern Ireland to take part in a Christian music festival weekend. This, to my surprise, was attended by an extremely large crowd in Belfast city centre. I had not been at such a meeting before. Then to my astonishment and surprise, I was asked to give my testimony at one of the meetings. I was happy to do so, though I was not accustomed to speaking in front of such a huge audience. I remember a gentleman, who I did not know very well, coming to speak to me afterwards to encourage me to do more speaking in the future. He said he was sure that I would become a recognised conference speaker in due course.

After attending the Bethany Hall for a couple of years, much as we enjoyed it, both my friend and I began to feel it was perhaps time to "move on". The main reason for this was that, for much of the time, we were the only two young people in the congregation. We both felt the need to have more fellowship with others in our age group. The elder I spoke to concerning what we were thinking about the future was, naturally, disappointed to see us leave but, nevertheless, could understand the reason for us doing so.

My friend decided to attend the Church of Scotland whose minister was involved in the seaside mission we attended. I decided to attend a small church instead that was very near to where I lived in Bridgeton. It was called the Zion Hall, and the minister was the main speaker at the 428 Club. Also, the group of people who were in my music group also attended this church, including my future wife, Janet. This seemed to be the best option for me, and I attended that church for several years and was most grateful to be welcomed as a full member of the church family.

It was here, through the encouragement of the pastor of the church, that I decided to be baptised by immersion. I did not want to do this till I was over eighteen years of age. This was because, at eighteen years of age, I would be recognised as an adult, and I would be responsible for my own decisions. My parents, for example, would be able to lay any blame squarely on my shoulders should anyone from the Muslim community raised any objections. I did not tell anyone from the family about my forthcoming baptism, as no member would have considered attending in any case.

I also wondered about changing my name. After all, "Riaz Mohammed" was not a very Christian sounding name! I was not sure if that was a good idea or not. As I was considering this possibility, I had to appear as a medical witness in court. As is the custom, I was offered a Bible to take into my hand and to swear to tell the truth. As I was about to speak, the judge spoke up and asked me if I would like to have the Koran instead of the Bible to swear by. I thanked the judge for his courtesy and said that, despite my name, I was a follower of Jesus Christ and happy to swear on the Bible. The judge was clearly astonished to hear this, as were many others in that courtroom. This occasion quite unexpectedly turned into an opportunity to witness because of my name. I decided not to change my name after that.

A year after I had qualified and become a doctor, my wife and I were able to buy a house in a place called Lenzie. This area was several miles from Bridgeton. We continued to attend the Zion Hall in Bridgeton as often as my clinical duties allowed. When, however, Mark was born, it became more difficult to attend on a regular basis. We began to wonder if going somewhere more local to worship would make more sense.

We discovered that our next-door neighbours in Lenzie were also Christians and had spent many years as missionaries in India. They attended the local Baptist church in Kirkintilloch, which was only a few miles away. They encouraged us to consider worshipping there. We took their advice and soon discovered the benefit of worshipping in a church in the area in which we lived.

Very soon, with our pastor's blessing, we joined the Kirkintilloch Baptist Church. From then on, we continued to be in membership in churches associated with the Baptist denomination. It just so happened that the art student through whose witness I had become a Christian at the school holiday camp had been a member of a Baptist church too.

Later, after being in membership at the Kirkintilloch Baptist Church for some time, I was privileged to be elected to the office of a deacon, which gave me some more insight into how a church was run. When the church membership decided to seek a second minister, I was asked to join the relevant committee chosen to find someone suitable for the post. We all felt that the Reverend Liam Goligher was the right person to join the pastoral team and were delighted when he accepted the nomination, and the church also accepted him as associate pastor.

This led to a wonderful time of growth for the Church. Liam was a gifted preacher, and it was wonderful to listen to him preaching every week. We all learnt a great deal from his teaching ministry. In addition, Janet and I got to know Liam and his wife, Christine, well. This too was a great privilege.

Liam, in time, went on to be recognised as a gifted preacher and began to be invited to preach at national conferences such as the annual Keswick Convention. It seemed obvious that he would move on from the church at Kirkintilloch.

We however had to leave before him. Whilst I was of course delighted to have been chosen for a consultant surgeon post in Dunfermline, it was a real loss to leave our home in Lenzie and Kirkintilloch Baptist Church. We had seen a mini-revival taking place under the preaching of Liam

Goligher. The church had become our family, and I particularly enjoyed meeting with male friends at each other's homes to study the scriptures in detail after the evening service on most Sunday nights. I would miss that engagement with others very much.

As I had to live within a ten-mile radius of the hospital, we had to move home and church. On our senior pastor's recommendation, we joined the Viewfield Baptist Church in Dunfermline.

On attending Viewfield Baptist Church, from my perspective, it felt as though we were going back in time. The way things were done in the church was not up to date, unlike the way our previous church was run. I did serve on the deacon's committee. But after about a year, because of some theological differences with the serving minister, I thought it best not to continue as a deacon.

We did get involved in an attempt to start a church plant in Crossford village where we lived, but there was not enough support or enthusiasm for this. And after a few years, the decision was made by the church to discontinue the services in the village.

We also started a home group meeting for the older members of the congregation. This we called the 40plus Group. We found that to be a great success, as many of the elderly members of the church were isolated from the rest of the fellowship. This group met every month on a Friday night for fellowship and supper.

For the younger and fitter members of the fellowship, we started a walking group on Saturdays. This was a great success, with many members of the church and many non-members coming along regularly. This was meant to be a pre-evangelism activity. We were overcome some months later when a lady was baptised in the church and, in her testimony, indicated that her faith started because of her being part of the walking group!

We worshipped in the Viewfield Baptist Church for the whole time we were in Dunfermline. Among others, Janet and I got to know the church organist very well. Sadly, he became very unwell and, after due investigations, was diagnosed with cancer of the lung. This was devastating for him and his family. In faith, he invited the minister and me to come to his home and pray for him. We went to his house and prayed that he would be healed. Thereafter, he underwent surgery to remove one of his lungs. He survived the operation and then went on to live for many years with no further evidence of recurrence of his cancer. It was wonderful to hear him play the organ and lead church worship once again.

We learnt from our experiences that, whilst no church was perfect, and indeed we were not perfect members either, nevertheless, being available to the Spirit of God to work in whatever capacity the Spirit chose always led to much blessing and satisfaction.

After about thirteen years in Dunfermline, we moved to Glasgow for me to work in the Victoria Infirmary, which was situated on the south of the River Clyde. It so happened that we had visited the Newton Mearns Baptist Church, which was close to the house we were in the process of buying.

When the hepatitis problem hit the media, the minister of the church telephoned me to reassure me that he and the elders of the church were praying for me. I was very encouraged by that phone call, and Janet and I determined that, when we moved to Glasgow, we would join the Newton Mearns Baptist Church.

We duly did so. And it transpired, sometime later, Janet was asked to join the pastoral team and served as the church administrator for several years, to her great satisfaction.

It was here, whilst worshipping in the Newton Mearns Baptist Church that the opportunity presented itself to consider some form of religious work abroad. The minister of our church had decided that it would be best to have some sort of relationship with a missionary organisation in India. This was because, whilst the church had contact with some Christian workers in Eastern Europe and Africa, there was no contact with anyone in Asia. The pastor took the view that the church should attempt some sort of Christian work in India too. He felt that I might be the best person to contact an organisation known as the Indian Rural Evangelical Fellowship (IREF). He and his wife had been in India working with the IREF some year previously and so thought that someone from the church going to India with them as our church representative would be worth considering.

I had been to India before as part of the examining team of the Royal College of Surgeons and Physicians of Glasgow and thought, rather naively, that it would not be a problem to go to India on behalf of the church and set up liaison with the IREF.

The Scottish representative of IREF was a dentist working in the Glasgow Dental Hospital. A meeting was set up between him and me to take things forward. He took the view that the medical work done by the group was very minor and basic. It consisted of recommending people seeing a GP for further medical care. He felt that, as a consultant surgeon, I would not have enough to do. However, the group also did several preaching engagements. His view was that, given my background, I could possibly assist with that aspect of the work instead. I was quite happy to assist in any way that I could. He then told me that this aspect of the work was in the hands of the Americans and that he would contact them so that I could be taken on to the preaching team. That seemed reasonable to me. So, I waited to receive further information from the United States. Despite waiting for quite a while, I received no expected emails.

Whilst waiting to hear from IREF, Janet and I went to visit my surgeon friend in Yorkshire. I shared the possible contact with IREF with him and explained that I was keen to go to India to represent the Church and, God willing, set up some form of contact with the churches there.

To my surprise, he told me he had been to India and had visited a Christian hospital known as the Duncan Hospital. This hospital was in a very poor area of India known as Bihar and was part of the Indian Emmanuel Hospital Association. It had been started by a Christian doctor named Cecil Duncan some seventy years ago. He suggested that, if things didn't work out with IREF, I might want to consider a visit to the Duncan Hospital instead! We could perhaps go together and consider taking a team of doctors with us to help them.

As I heard nothing at all from the United States, I decided that a visit to the Duncan Hospital was worth considering instead. The Hospital was in Raxaul, in Bihar, one of the poorest parts of India. Also, to make it even more interesting, it was situated on the border with Nepal and thus served the poor people of south Nepal as well. The way things worked there was that any person living in Nepal or India could cross the national boundary without any formal checks. This allowed people to come and go between the borders with no restrictions, thus allowing patients to come to the hospital as needed. After further discussion with my surgeon friend, it was decided that we would get a group together and make our way to the hospital for a short visit.

The problems I experienced in obtaining a visa to visit India was incredible! The only reason for this was that I had been born in Pakistan. Even though I had only been there for less than six years from birth and had British citizenship, nevertheless, this turned out to be a major difficulty. I had to get sponsors from India to send out an invitation for my visit. In addition, they had to give a written guarantee that they would be responsible for my conduct. I also had to submit information about my parents and grandparents, even though when they were all born, there was no such country as Pakistan.

Getting permission for a single-entry visa to India took several months. And during all this time the Indian government had my UK passport, which meant I could not travel anywhere else. Despite all this work, there was no guarantee I would be granted a visa at the end of the day. I had, nevertheless, to book and pay for my flight to India. And should a visa not be granted, I would simply have to forgo the plane ticket. Trying to obtain a visa to visit India made me feel as though I was a foreigner and a stranger in this world. I suppose, given the political differences between India and Pakistan, these kinds of things are to be expected. But I was sad to see that there was no discretion shown.

Meanwhile the other members of the team, all of whom were British, achieved a visa within a week of application.

Still, praise God, in the end, I was granted a visa and could fly into India with the rest of the team. The journey consisted of my flying into Schiphol Airport in Holland and meeting up with the rest of the team from England. We then flew into Delhi Airport. After staying overnight in Delhi, we all boarded the train to Raxaul. It was very interesting when we were asked by the porters of the hotel when they were loading the van to take us to the train station where we were going. When, we answered we were going to Raxaul, they were amazed. Even they said, "Raxaul? No one goes to Raxaul!"

The train journey from Delhi to Raxaul took over twenty-six hours and proved to be a very interesting train journey indeed. On the long ride, we came across several interesting people who came on and off the train very regularly. Every time the train stopped, the sellers of hot tea would come on! They then would get off the train as it started to move again.

As we were going to a large hospital, which was well known as a Christian-run hospital, we had, in addition to medical equipment, several Gideon Bibles to give away. We were instructed to make sure that the Bibles were all safely locked away in our suitcases. Nevertheless, I felt it was just right for me to take one of the Bibles in English, and keep it in my pocket, whilst the other Bibles were safely locked away. The reason for these feelings became clear later whilst on the train journey.

It so happened that an Indian gentleman joined us on the train for part of the journey. He, of course, noticed that I, an Asian-looking person, was friends with some "white English" people. After a while, he began to speak to me in a general kind of way. His spoken English was excellent. He asked me where we were going. I informed him that we were making our way, as a medical team, to the Duncan Hospital. He had heard of the Duncan Hospital and was very interested to learn why we were going there.

I told him that we were Christians and had come to India with a view to helping the poor of that area. One thing led to another, and the Indian gentleman told me that he was a teacher who, once a year, went by train to Delhi to buy some books. He was very interested in the various religions available in India. He knew Christianity was a recognised small religion in India but did not know much about it.

As he said this, I took out the Gideon Bible from my pocket and asked if he would be prepared to accept this as a gift. This book would be interesting reading for him and would tell him a little more about Christianity. He looked at it and opened the first page. He read out the words "not for sale" printed on the inside cover. He obviously could read and understand English. He accepted the gift of the Gideon Bible and carefully put it into his suitcase. A little while later, he said goodbye and left the train. We did not see him again. It was, however, wonderful that I had a Bible to give in my pocket. This was done without causing any disruption or drawing a great deal of attention by having to open a suitcase in public to take out a Bible to give away.

Bihar turned out to be as poor an area as we had imagined it to be. In many ways, it was like going back in time. However, the Duncan Hospital was truly like an oasis in a large desert area. We had a wonderful time at the hospital.

As I was not, by this time, in clinical surgery, it turned out that I did more preaching than medical work. This was with the help of an interpreter of course. I also spent some time with the senior staff, many of whom were able to speak English well. In addition to getting to know them in a personal manner, I was able to listen to them talking about the various burdens they were carrying. Given the social norms, where senior people had some difficulty in sharing their difficulties with those under their authority, it was good for them to share their concerns with a visitor such as me. It was also a privilege to support them in prayer.

One day, the chief executive saw me as he was going to a meeting with some local people. He was very concerned about the meeting and asked me to pray for him, as he was genuinely concerned for his safety.

This was because Duncan Hospital had been cooperating with the government to assist the very poor women who were being seen in the hospital for maternal care. As postnatal infection was very common and antibiotics were often required by these women and their newborn babies, this led to a major problem for the very poor. They could not afford to pay for the antibiotics. They would either accept whatever would happen to their health or alternatively go into serious debt to pay for expensive antibiotic treatment.

The chief executive had agreed with the government that, given the proven status of these women, namely that they were so poor they could not afford to buy the necessary antibiotics, these women, and these only, would receive free antibiotics from the hospital. Some of this information had obviously gotten out into the community, and many locals were not at all pleased with the arrangement.

It transpired that several local stallholders had become accustomed to selling antibiotics at reduced price to patients from the hospital. These stall owners, who all had their stalls out in the street next to the hospital, were very concerned that this new agreement would ruin their trade. Hence, they came for a meeting with the chief executive to demand some sort of compromise. They were potentially violent, and the life of the chief executive was in real danger.

It was also a well-known fact that these sellers of antibiotics were not in any way qualified, and many of the antibiotics sold in the marketplace were not antibiotics at all. Unfortunately, the poor could not read and would simply buy whatever they were given, as it was cheaper than the normal price they would have to pay.

We went off immediately to get down on our knees and start praying. The chief executive did not want anyone else in the meeting, as he felt that this could give rise to even more trouble.

One policeman turned up with a rifle, and the meeting went ahead in his presence. The chief executive explained honestly what the Duncan Hospital had agreed with the government, and because this was clearly of great help to the very poor pregnant women, he refused to withdraw this arrangement. The hospital, he said, would continue to serve these poor women in this way. But he did say that this was a voluntary arrangement with the very poor pregnant women and no other patients. All other patients did not have this arrangement in place and were free to purchase antibiotics from wherever they wished.

The meeting, I was told later, ended with the stall owners accepting that this was not unreasonable. There then followed handshakes all round. The chief executive was very grateful for our prayers, as the potential for a violent outcome was very real indeed. That's the way things were in Bihar.

We also discovered that the old buildings of the hospital were becoming less functional and passed repairable. They also tended to be flooded regularly during the rainy season. The hospital managers had, therefore, sought funding to start a new hospital building on a nearby site. They had managed to start the project. But after the foundations and some walls had been built, they had run out of money, and the building project had come to a complete halt.

This situation was not good! Many people, including some of the staff, were beginning to feel that the wrong decision had been made by the senior management. They were now worse off than before. They had spent a great deal of the money gifted by people from all around the world on the new building, yet not a single patient had been treated there. Some clearly thought the money could have been put to better use. We took the view that building a new hospital was perfectly reasonable and would serve the community very well for years to come.

We decided that the best way we could help the staff was to raise money to finish the building when we got home.

My money-raising venture did not go at all well. Despite writing to several well-known multimillionaires, who gave substantial amounts of money to charity, no one was interested in helping to complete a building, even though it was to be a hospital for the poor. This was very disappointing.

I also wrote a short article about our visit to the Duncan Hospital for publication in the Medical and Dental Defence Union of Scotland journal, which is sent to all general practitioners in the United Kingdom. The article, basically, gave a factual account of what was happening in that part of the world. I thought that this article would be of some interest to the general practitioners in the United Kingdom.

To my surprise, I received a phone call from a retired GP after he had read the article. He, it turned out, had been a missionary together with his wife, who was also a doctor, at the Duncan Hospital for over ten years. They had to come back to Scotland to look after elderly parents.

Having read my article, he felt the need to get in touch with me, as he wanted to do something more for the hospital. This was very encouraging. He and his wife joined in with several other people, who also had developed an interest in the hospital, giving birth to a group that became to be known as the "Friends of the Duncan Hospital". We began to meet regularly to pray and support the hospital.

One day, Joanna, who was the wife of the GP, happened to meet up with a family friend. She had been very friendly with his mother, who sadly died of breast cancer when he was very young. He was by now a consultant orthopaedic surgeon.

He told Joanna that he was thinking of buying a local professional football club. Joanna, who later admitted that this did not mean very much to her, as she did not know much about football, just happened to say that he would be better off spending his money on something more useful, such as helping the poor people at the Duncan Hospital in India.

This struck a totally unexpected cord with her friend. He listened to what Joanna had said and decided that he would like to send a gift to the Duncan Hospital instead of buying the football club.

Joanna approached me to see if I could advise how a gift of money could be sent to Duncan Hospital. She thought her friend would send a few thousand pounds for the hospital building fund. We were, by this time, accustomed to sending monetary gifts through the Edinburgh Medical and Missionary Society, now known as EMMS (International), as this was a safe and easy way of doing so. I thus gave the necessary information to Joanna and then thought not much more about it. I was too busy trying to see how large funds could be obtained to finish the hospital building.

The following day, I received a phone call from the chief executive of EMMS (International) to tell me that something unexpected and very unusual had happened. They had been asked to forward, as a gift, the sum of £500,000 for the Duncan Hospital Building Project. This was the biggest single gift they had ever received. It was a huge amount of money for all of us in the United Kingdom but equivalent to very much more for India. This was utterly amazing and totally unexpected for us all.

The sum given was more than enough to complete the hospital project. The orthopaedic surgeon, together with his wife, went to the opening ceremony of the hospital and continued to have an interest in raising funds for the hospital. Very shortly thereafter, poor patients began to be treated in an excellent modern hospital building. This was indeed an answer to prayer.

Whilst the visit to India through IREF did not work out, as often happens, God had a bigger and better plan, which no one had even thought about. How great is our God!

When we moved to Edinburgh, we joined the Charlotte Baptist Chapel. This is a very large church in the city centre. Our pastor in Newton Mearns thought this would suit us very well. As it so happened, it was quite close to where Mark now lived and reasonably near to our grandson Ethan, who lived with his mother. I thought it might be wise to join this church as advised. Hopefully, when I was allowed, I could bring either grandchild to church.

It was interesting to be in a very large city centre church with many foreign members from all over the world. After a while as members of the church, I was asked to serve as an elder and did so for a few years. One of the reasons I was asked to take on the role of an elder was that I was a foreigner. Given that all the other elders up to that time were white men, the pastor was keen for me to assist in this way. At least on this occasion being a foreigner and stranger in this world was of some benefit to someone.

Over the years, whilst in membership of these churches, I continued to preach wherever I was invited to do so. My wife would often accompany me and sing solo as another way of telling the story of salvation.

Whilst in membership at the Newton Mearns Baptist Church, I was asked to join the committee of the Scottish Baptist Lay Preachers Association. This is an association of lay preachers who are recognised by the Baptist Union as being adequately trained to assist churches needing preachers. This became another avenue through which I would receive invitations to preach and give my testimony in Baptist and other evangelical churches in all kinds of circumstances. It was also of interest to find out that the first meeting of the SBLPA took place, some seventy years earlier, at the Charlotte Baptist chapel where Janet and I are now in membership. It's a small world!

Over the years, we began to discover that there was no such thing as a perfect church. Someone gave the advice that, "If you find a perfect church, consider not joining it, as you would immediately stop it being perfect." How true! Nevertheless, over the years I discovered that the church indeed was the body of Christ, of which He was the head. I found from my own experience that I was more accepted into the family in the church than anywhere else in the world.

It remains the case however, no matter how long I have lived in the United Kingdom that people will often ask me, "Where do you come from?" Having lived in Scotland for over sixty years, which often is more than those who ask me the question; it still makes me feel like a foreigner and stranger.

In addition, having become a Christian, there would be no value in returning to the country of my birth! It is a strong possibility that I might even be considered worthy of severe punishment and even death for denying Islam. So, the feeling of being a foreigner and a stranger would be even more real there than anywhere else! All that I can now do is to look forward to that day when I will be going to my true home in heaven forever.

CONCLUSION

There are many, many questions in life for which, at least for me, there are no easy answers. Why was I brought from a third-world country to the Western World at a very young age when I had no choice? My parents, without doubt, did so in my best interests. But God would have known the consequences of such a move. God must have known that this move, and my subsequent experiences, would make me feel a stranger and foreigner all my life. Certainly, there were times when life seemed to be worth living, but these times did not last very long. They were soon replaced by sad times, taking me back into my feelings of not belonging.

I often wonder whether, if my family had not migrated to the United Kingdom, would I still have become a Christian? Or would I have remained a Muslim worshipping in the same manner as the rest of my family? If the latter had been the case, would I then not be given entry into heaven, as I would not have had Jesus Christ as my saviour? These theoretical questions can't really be answered. Only God has all the answers.

Why has my life been so difficult and painful in many ways? Surely God could have made it a little easier? Then again you might argue, there are many others in this world whose lives are, and will continue to be, a lot more difficult than mine! Does God always intervene in their lives?

Why and how did I acquire hepatitis B, which, at the end of the day, cost me my career in surgery? Did I get it in Pakistan as a child or was it acquired from a patient? Interestingly, none of my brothers have had hepatitis B. This was confirmed by testing their blood samples. If I had acquired it from my mother at birth, at least one of them would also have acquired hepatitis B.

The question remains, what does the future hold for me? Will I develop cirrhosis of the liver, which can then lead to cancer of the liver? No one can know for sure. I attend regularly my consultant infectious diseases outpatient clinic and have an ultrasound scan of my liver on a regular basis. Apart from some fatty infiltration of my liver, all seems normal. I must just live with what I have.

As I ask these questions of God, I am conscious that God replies, just as he did many years ago, by asking me a question in return as His answer. The answer God continues to give is simply this: "Do you trust me or not?"

A positive answer to this question is crucial for a life of faith now. The other questions will all be answered but not necessarily in this life!

What remains sure, as far as I am concerned, is that for now, I will continue to be nothing other than a foreigner and stranger in this world till that day dawns and the shadows flee away. I look forward to that day when I will finally be going to my heavenly home! Home will be all the sweeter given my present experience.

I wonder where you, as a reader of this autobiography, stand as far as faith in Jesus Christ is concerned. Do you hold the view that my experiences of life simply reflect what happens to some people and my experience is not much different from others? Is it the case that I am just imagining things and God has not intervened in my life at all? I have no way to prove beyond all doubt that God has acted with love and grace in my life and that He will do the same for you if you put your trust in His saving grace. The only way to find out is to do just what I have done— namely, give your life into His divine hands. If you choose to do so, you will, I believe, be amazed to see God work in your life in a way that is relevant to you and your situation and not just a copy of mine. The latter would just be useless in any case.

My reason for writing this autobiography is to point to Jesus Christ, in the hope that the reader will be encouraged to put his or her trust in Him too. I have no way of knowing if I have succeeded in doing so. But my prayer is that, if God wills, someone will be encouraged take that leap of faith.

In the meanwhile, thanks to His mercy and grace, I continue to live for His glory. I thank God daily for my wife, for my family, and for the people of God—without whom life would not be worth living.

Finally, my prayer remains consistently the same: "Come soon, Lord Jesus, and take your servant home."

SOME THOUGHTS ON FAITH AND RELIGION

There are many people in the world today who do not believe in the existence of God. Their view often seems to be that everything that there is has come into being just by chance. There is no meaning to life except whatever meaning we give it, and after death, existence comes to an end, and there is nothing.

This view, though it is becoming more common, is contrary to what is taught in the Bible. The Bible makes it abundantly clear that everything that we see and know, everything that exists, did not come about simply be chance but was deliberately created by God and is sustained by God. Furthermore, this world will not continue forever. But when God decides the time is right, this world will come to an end and will be replaced by another creation. Also, after death, humankind will be judged by God, who will decide if a person will face eternity with or without Him.

How does one decide which opinion to follow, as the two views are clearly incompatible? If one goes for the view that everything happened by chance, then one must answer the question, what is chance? How did chance come about? From where did the elements of protons, electrons, primordial cells and tissues originate? How did the laws of nature, which appear to be consistent, regulated, and stable, come about? Answers to these questions must remain unanswered, apart from saying that all these things must have happened just by chance.

The God view is also open to difficulty. Where did God come from? How did He create all that there is? The Bible does not answer the question about the origin of God, except to say that God has always been there. He has no "beginning" and has no "end". He is above and beyond anything that humanity can ever understand. So, if one chooses to go down the "God route", then one must believe that God exists and that He rewards those who seek Him.

As for those who decide to go down the "no God-only chance route", then each person must rely on chance as to what happens. If those who choose this path are right and there is no God, then I suppose they are no worse off. And, I suspect, those who are believers are probably no worse off either. If, however, they are wrong and there is a God, then they must give an account of their position to their creator. I can only wish them "luck"! For if one chooses not to believe in the existence of the living God, when he does in fact exist, then this can only bring one great difficulty on the Day of Judgement.

A person who believes in a God of some kind but fails to recognise that the only route to salvation, according to the Bible, is through Jesus Christ, the God-man would also face great difficulty.

Some people, including some Christians, have difficulty with the tale of creation as written by the prophet Moses in the book known as Genesis. After all, it is often argued, given the scientific knowledge we now have acquired, how can things be created in a day? Some things that have been discovered are millions of years old. How do these scientific facts fit with the biblical narrative?

Whilst it is difficult to answer all these reasonable questions, it is worth thinking a little "outside of the box"! For example, we must not put God under, and subject to, time. We are subjects of time, but God is not. He is above and outside of time. To Him, one thousand years could be no longer than one day.

If we take, for example, a very large tree that is present in front of us, we can scientifically examine it. And from all our experience, using all the verified rules we have, we may conclude—as agreed and verified by all—that the tree in question is, say, seventy-five years old. However, in God's ultimate reality, God just says let the tree appear, and it does so. It would take God, who is not governed by time, only a second to make it happen. So, in God's reality the tree is, in fact, one second old, not seventy-five years old. Both ways of looking are "correct", providing we understand what we are doing. Of course, if one chooses to believe that God does not exist, then the only available option is that the tree is seventy-five years old.

Or, take for example, the coming to life of Adam, the first man. I would imagine, if we looked at Adam when he first appeared in the Garden of Eden, from a scientific point of view, we may come to a reasonable scientific conclusion that he was, say, for the sake of argument, twenty years old. However, we would simply be wrong, for in God's reality, Adam was only one day old. This would mean that the scientific method, governed by time, would be wrong by a factor equal to $1 \times 7,300$. This way of thinking does, however, require faith to believe that God is and has the power to do things not possible for humankind.

When we look a little further into the creation of Adam and Eve, we might ask the question: Why did God make Adam first? Why not make Eve first? Well, we know now a little more about genetics than was known in the days of Moses. We now know that the sex genes that a man has are called the X and Y chromosomes, whereas the female has only X chromosomes.

If one starts with a female, then it would be possible to produce other humans, by cloning the sex chromosomes and then using two of the X chromosomes to bring about another person. However, that would mean the other person would also be female. If, however, one can clone the genes from a male, then two X chromosomes can be brought together to make a female, as well as bringing an X and Y chromosome together to make another male.

Furthermore, we now know a little more about stem cells from which other genes can be cloned—hence, the existence of Dolly the sheep! We know further that these stem cells can be isolated from bone marrow, which can be found in a rib. Is this why God, after putting Adam into a deep sleep (anaesthesia), took a rib and then used the stem cells from the bone marrow to bring together two of Adams X chromosomes to form Eve?

Another crucial issue concerns the nature of God. It is true that the monotheistic religions—Judaism, Christianity, and Islam—all believe in one God. However, there is often some misunderstanding, particularly around the Christian idea of "one God". Some believe that the Christians have not one but three gods, as God is spoken of as God the Father, God the Son, and God the Holy Spirit.

This is simply a misunderstanding, although for those who do not know what the Bible states, it is an easy mistake to make. The plain fact is that, like Judaism before it, Christians believes in only one God. The difference is that there is more self-revelation of God by God Himself in the New Testament. It is God who revels Himself in this manner. It is not an invention by the church. It just would not be possible to invent such a thing as the Trinity in Unity, nor any necessity to do so.

The reason this belief is held is simply because God has told us more of what He is like. Furthermore, it is quite clear that, whilst man is made in the image of God, the reverse is not true. God is not made in the image of man. God is Spirit, and He is a much more complex being than man is or can be. It is God who has chosen to reveal himself in a triune way. Who is man to say to God that he cannot do that?

It is, in fact, impossible to fully understand the "Trinity in Unity" aspect of the Christian faith. But not to fully understand God should come as no surprise to humankind. We, as Christians, believe in the Unity of the Trinity because the Bible teaches us that that is the case. Thus, we believe this truth because God has chosen to reveal this aspect of His character to humankind.

Another major difficulty arises when one considers who Jesus is and what the Bible says about him. Whilst some of what the Bible says about Jesus is attested to in the Koran, which only became available some 650 years after the actual event, there are significant differences—which, in my view, need to be faced by all.

The Bible makes it abundantly clear that Jesus Christ was crucified on the cross by the Roman soldiers until he died. Further, the Bible teaches that Jesus died, not for any sin he himself had committed, as he was perfect and free of all sin, but to pay the price of the sin of humankind. He was then raised back to life on the third day, as the full price of sin was fully paid. This unique historical fact was attested to not only by his apostles, most of whom died sharing this Good News with others, but also by more than five hundred other people who also saw Jesus after he was raised from the dead.

The reason Jesus had to die for humankind's sin is that humankind is sinful by nature, and there was no other solution to the problem of getting rid of sin forever except through the redemption brought about by Jesus. This is because Adam and Eve sinned in the Garden of Eden, and as a direct result of this, every one of us is born sinful and prone to sin. This teaching of the Bible is contradicted by others, including Islam. Islam religion teaches that humankind is born sinless, and we become sinful by our disobedience to God, which can be prevented by following Islam. Hence, there is no reason for Jesus to die on the Cross.

If one believes that we cannot be sinless and need a saviour such as Jesus, which is the belief required of all Christians, then the question arises: How can it be that an ordinary human being, even if this person were a prophet of God, could pay the price of sin for the whole of humanity and for all time just by one death on the Cross? Also, the price is paid by his death in three days, and he does not suffer thereafter. So, if the price for the sin of humankind has been fully paid then, surely, only someone as great as God alone could pay that price. This is precisely what the Bible says about Jesus, who was God in human form. He was fully God and fully man. We cannot fully understand how that can be possible, but then, we are out of our territory of knowledge and understanding. These matters, in the end, belong only to God. Not even the angels and heavenly beings can fully understand it all.

The other issue that Muslims and Christians must face concerns the death of Jesus on the Cross itself. The Koran says that Jesus was not crucified on the Cross, as God would not let his prophet go through such a dreadful death. So, to fool the Jews and the Romans into thinking they had crucified Jesus, God blinded them all, so they thought they had crucified Jesus when, in fact, they crucified someone else who was made to look like Jesus to them. Jesus was not killed on the Cross and was taken up into heaven without dying.

The Bible makes it completely clear that Jesus Himself was the substitute, which, for example, Abraham's story foretells. In Abraham's case, the life of his son Isaac was saved because God provided a ram as a substitute. Now God provides himself as the lamb in the form of the God-man Jesus, who saves us all.

This, in my view, is such a crucial difference between what the Koran teaches and what the Bible teaches that a decision must be made as to which view one should accept. Both cannot be true.

If one accepts the Bible as the word of God, which made this theological truth available to humankind centuries before the Koran became available, why would one choose to believe a completely different story? Why would God, who is the God of truth, make people believe a lie for centuries before revealing the truth?

Looking a little further into the book of Genesis, we find that, in the centre of the Garden of Eden, there were two trees. One that was forbidden for humankind to eat from was known as the tree of the knowledge of good and evil. The other, which was freely available to humankind, was the tree of life. If Adam and Eve had eaten of that tree, they would have lived forever. They were given the freedom to do so until they were removed from the Garden of Eden after sinning. This was done in order to prevent them from having access to the tree of life and, so, live forever!

However, when we consider the future, when God makes a new heaven and earth, as indicated in the last book of the Bible, known as Revelation, we find that there are not one but two trees of life (Revelation 22:2). There is one on either side of the river of life. There is no tree of the knowledge of good and evil. So, humankind can never fall and become sinful again. Hence, the saved will be with God forever!

Where did the other tree of life come from? Could it be the case that the Cross of Christ, which was the tree of death to him, became the new tree of life to those who put their faith in His death and resurrection?

Whatever one believes is the truth concerning the death of Jesus on the Cross helps to determine which religious faith one should follow. Whichever book we take as being the true word of God obviously determines what we put our faith and trust in. There are many similarities in the teaching of the two books, but these differences are crucial.

I take the view that these genuine questions of belief and faith should be discussed honestly, truthfully, humbly, and courteously with others, with a view to convincing others of the truth each person holds. I do not believe anyone should be forcefully made to believe any truth that one holds, no matter how important one considers that truth to be. I totally and utterly reject the use of force in any form, both physical and psychological, from any source, to "convert" others to one's own faith, whatever that faith happens to be. Each person must be allowed to make his or her own decision as to which faith to follow. After all, we will all have to answer to God for our actions.

I believe and preach that Christ is the only way to salvation based on what the Bible teaches. The church should teach and live this truth as a priority, even though in the providence of God, which is beyond human comprehension, only the Spirit of God ultimately brings about saving faith in Christ to repentant and believing hearts.

THE MOHAMMED FAMILY AT SYLVIA'S WEDDING

THE 'INCOMPLETE' DUNCAN HOSPITAL

COMPLETED DUNCAN HOSPITAL

Lightning Source UK Ltd.
Milton Keynes UK
UKHW012201290120
357834UK00001B/88

9 781973 668800